QUEST
FOR
ENLIGHTENMENT

The Quest for Enlightenment is a vast reservoir of quotations that were gleaned from various sources over the years. Personal growth depends on the intuitive feeling in our hearts which leads us to right understanding, and ultimately, to the enlightenment of the self. This impressive collection, which is a source of great inspiration, will help us in our search for enlightenment.

QUEST
FOR
ENLIGHTENMENT

*The quintessence of wisdom of over
five thousand years culled from nearly
three thousand books in a study lasting
fifty-six years devoted to portraying
the beauty, truth, and joy of life*

Compiled and Edited by
O.P. GHAI

Foreword by
DR. KARAN SINGH

A Sterling Paperback

STERLING PAPERBACKS
An imprint of
Sterling Publishers (P) Ltd.
L-10, Green Park Extension, New Delhi-110016

Quest for Enlightenment
©1997, Sterling Publishers Private Limited
ISBN 81 207 1728 7

Published by Sterling Publishers Pvt. Ltd., New Delhi-110016.
Lasertypeset by Vikas Compographics, New Delhi.
Printed at Ram Printograph, New Delhi-110051.
Cover design by Data Point

Contents

The End of a Quest

One day you walked away leaving us staring at the void.

Our arms shall dangle in vain unable to reach you in your kingdom of the far away stars.

Now you will weave the stars, clouds, sun and moon into a new alphabet of words and wisdom, print them on the pages of the blue sky and publish them through the sailing clouds.

While you were living, you united us with your words.

Now that you are gone, your long arms fold up our country into a cartographic oneness in your silken embrace.

You gave the dumb author a tongue and the anonymous face a name.

The books you fathered celebrate your memories like pyramids on the sprawling desolation of our silence.

Whenever we go in quest of excellence, achievement, inspiration or development on the highways of our minds, we shall meet you coming back with stretched arms still exploring, still questing, still striving, still blessing us with raindrops of pure love falling from your domed abode with the limitless bounty of your boundless heart.

A tribute by MAN MOHAN SINGH
Former Resident Financial Commissioner,
Panjab Government

Foreword

Shri O.P. Ghai was a man who combined professional excellence with a deep commitment to moral and ethical values. In the course of a long and creative life, he gathered a vast reservoir of quotations from the great classics of the world, on the basis of which he brought out several volumes devoted to different themes.

This useful work has been continued by his son Shri S.K. Ghai, and the latest in the series is a remarkable collection entitled *Quest for Enlightenment*. Spiritual realisation has been the main goal before all the great religions of the world, although they may have prescribed different paths to reach it. This impressive collection will, I am sure, be a source of great inspiration to serious seekers and educationists not only in India but throughout the world.

Dr. Karan Singh

Publisher's Note

My father, Shri O.P. Ghai, was a voracious reader during his lifetime. He had this peculiar trait of underlining meaningful passages and read them time and again. During his last few years, he wanted to share these selections with others which gave birth to a fine series of four books—Quest for the Fine Art of Living: *Quest for Achievement, Quest for Development, Quest for Inspiration* and *Quest for Excellence.* He also started compiling quotations and well-known sayings for *Quest for Perfection* and *Quest for Enlightenment.* While the work was in progress, he breathed his last on 6 May 1992. Picking up the thread, Vijaya Kumar has helped to fulfil his mission by filling in the gaps that were left behind him.

I am grateful to Dr. Karan Singh for writing the foreword and to Swami Gokulanandaji for his message.

S.K. Ghai

Message

There are many kinds of gems in this world, but *Quest for Enlightenment* by Shri O.P. Ghai is rather a gem of a different kind altogether. We deeply appreciate the efforts made by Shri S.K. Ghai, Managing Director of Sterling Publishers Pvt. Ltd., to bring out this valuable book of his illustrious father. *Quest for Enlightenment* is indeed a commendable work of Shri O.P. Ghai — the latest in the series of his earlier books — *Quest for Excellence, Quest for Achievement, Quest for Development* and *Quest for Inspiration.*

This book, *Quest for Enlightenment,* contains spiritually elevating messages from various religious texts of the world, as also the observations, sayings and utterances of some of the greatest saints, authors, poets and philosophers. All these have been sorted out in ten chapters under appropriate titles, so that one can read a chapter of his own choice at any time. The remarkable feature of this book is that even if one starts reading with a disturbed mind, a reading of one or two pages of this book will enable him to be conscious of the high dimension of his nature and thus be in tune with his real self. I wish the book wide circulation.

I have no doubt that this book will serve as a *vademecum* to all who strive for enlightenment.

Swami Gokulananda
Secretary, Ramakrishna Mission
New Delhi

GOD

How shall I speak of Thee?
How shall I praise Thee?
How shall I describe Thee?
How shall I know Thee?
Every one pretends to know of
Thee; O Lord; each bolder than
the other in his claim.
All I say is, God is great,
so   is   His   Name;
what He ordains comes to be.
                              —Guru Nanak

Each in His Own Tongue

A fire mist and a planet—
A crystal and a cell,—
A jelly first and a saurian,
And caves where the cavemen dwell;
Then a sense of law and beauty,
And a face turned from the clod—
Some call it Evolution,
And others call it God.

A haze on the far horizon,
The infinite, tender sky,
The ripe, rich tint of cornfields,
And the wild geese sailing high;
And all over upland and lowland
The charm of the golden rod—
Some of us call it Autumn,
And others call it God.

Like tides on a crescent sea beach,
When the moon is new and thin,
Into our hearts high yearnings
Come welling and surging in—
Come from the mystic ocean,
Whose rim no foot has trod—
Some of us call it Longing,
And others call it God.

A picket frozen on duty,
A mother starved for her brood,
Socrates drinking the hemlock,
And Jesus on the rood;
And millions who, humble and nameless,

The straight, hard pathway plod—
Some call it Consecration
And others call it God.

—*William Herbert Carruth*

My God, Thou art my All

My God, Thou art my Guide
A wanderer in a dark and desert land,
    A stranger on a tempest-beaten strand,
My Father, lead me with a gentle hand;
    Thou art my Guide.

My God, Thou art my Shield
In the fierce fight, amid un-numbered foes,
    Assailed by fierce darts and furious blows,
Beneath Thy shelter I can safe repose.
    Thou art my Shield.

My God, Thou are my Life
Thy breath has made the lifeless breathe alive,
    Thy quickening spirit doth all things revive,
Thou to Thy flock do'st life eternal give;
    Thou art my Life.

My God, Thou are my All
My first, my last, my Father and Friend;
    The Providence do'th all my way attend,
To Thee be glory, now and without end;
    Thou are my All.

—*Unknown*

I can see that in the midst of death, life persists; in the midst of untruth, truth persists. God is Life, Truth, Light. He is Love. He is the Supreme God. God is Conscience. He is the searcher of hearts. He transcends speech and reason. He knows us and our hearts better than we do ourselves.

God is personal to those who need his personal presence. He is embodied to those who need his touch. He is all things to all men. He is in us and yet beyond us.

—Mahatma Gandhi

God promises you His forgiveness and bounties; and God cares for all and He knows all things. He grants wisdom to whom He pleases, and he to whom wisdom is granted receives indeed a benefit overflowing; but none will grasp the Message but men with understanding

—Qur'an

Lord! You are the uninvoked Saviour, motiveless compassionate Being, a Wellwisher even when unprayed, a Friend even when unrelated

Vitaragastava

We, who live in the world still attached to *karmas*, can overcome the world by Thy grace alone.

Srimad Bhagavatam

Thou who pervadest all the worlds below,
    yet sitest above,
Master of all who work and rule and know,
    servant of Love !
Thou who disdainest not the worm to be
    Not even the clod,
Therefore we know by that humility
    That Thou art God.

—Sri Aurobindo

The Lord is my Shepherd

The Lord is my shepherd.
I shall not want;
He makes me lie down in
green pastures.
He leads me beside still
waters.
He restores my soul.
He leads me in paths of
righteousness
for His name's sake.
Even though I walk
through the valley of the
shadow of death.
I fear no evil,
for Thou art with me;
Thy rod and Thy staff
they comfort me.
Thou preparest a table
before me
in the presence of my enemies;
Thou anointest my head
with oil; my cup overflows
Surely goodness and mercy
shall follow me
all the days of my life;
and I shall dwell in the
house of the Lord for ever.

—Psalm 23

Who can sing Him, who taketh away life and again restoreth it?
Who can sing Him, who appeareth to be far, but is known to be near ?
Who can sing Him, who is all seeing and omnipresent ?
In describing Him there would never be an end.
Millions of men give millions upon millions of descriptions of Him, but they fail to describe Him.
The Giver giveth; the receiver groweth weary of receiving.
In every age man subsisteth by His bounty.
The Commander by His order hath laid out the world.
Nanak, God the unconcerned is happy.

—Guru Nanak

He is Allah, the Creater, the Shaper out of naught, the Fashioner. His are the most beautiful names. All that is in the Heavens and the Earth glorifyeth Him, and He is the Mighty, the Wise.
    So glorify the name of the Tremendous Lord.

—Qur'an

That which is most subtle in matter is air, in air the soul, in the soul intelligence, in intelligence God.

—Hermes

The doctrine of this supreme Presence is a cry of joy and exaltation. What man seeing this can lose it from his thought or entertain a meaner subject?

—Emerson

God is love, and he that dwelleth in love, dwelleth in God and God in him.

—John

God and His Power

Every gentle gale that blows,
   Every little stream that flows,
Through the green and flowery vale,
   Every flower that scents the gale,
Every soft refreshing shower,
   Sent upon the drooping flower,
Every tempest rushing by,
   Says to man that God is nigh.

Lofty hills with forest crowned,
   Deserts where no tree is found,
Rivers, from the mountain's source,
   Winding on their fruitful course,
Ocean with its mighty waves,
   Rocks and sands, and pearly caves,
All that in the ocean dwell,
   Unto us His goodness tell.

Every little creeping thing,
   Every insect on the wing,
Every bird that warbling flies
   Freely through his native skies,
Beasts that far from man abide
   Those that gambol by his side,
Cattle on a thousand hills,
   Say that God creation fills.

He has taught, with wonderous art,
   Each to act his proper part;
Food and shelter how to gain,
   How to guard itself from pain;
Makes its own existence bright,
   While it serves for man's delight,
All these creatures every hour
   Speak of God, and show His power.

—Unknown

7

We thank Thee, Lord

We thank Thee, Lord, for this fair earth,
  The glittering sky, the silver sea;
For all their beauty, all their worth,
  Their light and glory, come from Thee.

From Thee the flowers that clothe the ground,
  The trees that wave their arms above,
The hills that gird our dwellings round,
  As Thou do'st gird Thine own with love.

Yet teach us still how far more fair,
  More glorious, Father, in Thy sight,
Is one pure deed, one holy prayer,
  One heart that owns Thy Spirit's might.

So while we gaze, with thoughtful eye,
  On all the gifts Thy love has given,
Help us in our thoughts to rise,
  From this earth to glorious heaven.

—*Unknown*

Lord, when I look upon mine own life it seems Thou hast led me so carefully, so tenderly Thou canst have attended to no one else; but when I see how wonderfully Thou hast led the world and art leading it, I am amazed that Thou has time to attend to such as I.

—*St. Augustine*

Hard Refusals

My desires are many and my cry is pitiful, but ever didst Thou save me by hard refusals; and this strong mercy has been wrought into my life through and through.

Day by day Thou art making me worthy of the simple, great gifts that Thou gavest to me unasked—this sky and the light, this body and the life and the mind—saving me from perils of overmuch desire.

There are times when I languidly linger and times when I awaken and hurry in search of my goal; but cruelly Thou hidest Thyself from before me.

Day by day Thou art making me worthy of Thy full acceptance by refusing me ever and anon, saving me from perils of weak, uncertain desire.

—*Rabindranath Tagore*

God guides best, when He tempts worst, loves entirely when He punishes cruelly, helps perfectly when violently He opposes.

—*Sri Aurobindo*

I know that I have in me something without which nothing could be. It is that I call God.

—*Angelus Silesius*

Wide open to all beings be the gates of the Everlasting.

—*Mahavagga*

9

What God hath promised

God hath not promised
  Skies always blue,
Flower-strewn pathways
  All our lives through;
God hath not promised
  Sun without rain,
Joy without sorrow,
  Peace without pain.

But God hath promised
  Strength for the day,
Rest for the labor,
  Light for the way,
Grace for the trials,
  Help from above,
Unfailing sympathy,
  Undying love.

—*Annie Johnson Flint*

O son of earth, be blind and thou shalt see My beauty; be deaf
and thou shalt hear My sweet song, My pleasant melody; be
ignorant and thou shalt partake My knowledge; be in distress and thou shalt have an eternal portion of the infinite
ocean of My riches: —blind to all that is not My beauty, deaf
to all that is not My word, ignorant of all that is not My
knowledge. Thus with a gaze that is pure, a spirit without
stain, and understanding refined, thou shalt enter into my
sacred presence.

—*Baha-ullah*

God is Love

God is Love; His mercy brightens
All the paths in which we rove;
Bliss He wakes and woe He lightens
God is wisdom, God is love

Chance and change are busy ever;
Man decays, and ages move;
But His mercy waneth never;
God is wisdom, God is love.

E'en the hour that darkest seemeth,
Will His changeless goodness prove;
From the gloom his brightness streameth,
God is wisdom, God is love.

He with earthly cares entwineth
Hope and comfort from above;
Everywhere His glory shineth;
God is wisdom, God is love.

—*John Browning*

He was Eternal before Time was born,
He was Eternal when Time began to run its course,
He is even now Eternal, and
He will be Eternal for all times to come.

—*Japji*

God has explained one thing to me,
That there is but one Lord of all creation,
and I should not forget him.

—*Guru Nanak*

In the beginning was the Word and the Word was with God, and the Word was God. The same was in the beginning with God. All things were made by Him; and without Him was not anything made that was made. In Him was life; and the life was the light of men. And the light shineth in darkness; and the darkness comprehendeth it not.

—*Gospel of St. John*

I make and unmake this universe. Apart from Me nothing exists, O Arjuna. All things, like the beads of a necklace, are strung together on the thread of My consciousness, and are sustained by me.

—*Bhagavad Gita*

"I am the fluidity of water. I am the silver light of the moon and the golden light of the sun. I am the *Aum* chanted in all the Vedas: the Cosmic Sound moving, as if soundlessly, through the ether. I am the manliness of men. I am the good sweet smell of the moist earth. I am the luminescence of fire; the sustaining life of all living creatures. I am self-offering in those who would expand their little lives into cosmic life. O Arjuna, know Me as the Eternal Seed of all creatures. In the perceptive, I am their perception. In the great, I am their greatness. In the glorious, it is I who am their glory."

—*Bhagavad Gita*

Believe in God, For He is Perfect
In Knowledge and Power, forgives Sin
And Accepts Repentance, and justly
Enforces His Law. Those who reject Him
Are but in deceit: His glory is sung
By the highest and purest. Give all devotion
To Him alone. The Day of Requital
Is ever drawing near, when Falsehood
Will vanish, and God's Truth and Justice
Will be established for all Eternity.

—*Qur'an*

As the same fish is dressed into the soup, curry or cutlet, and each man has his own choice of the dish of it, so the Lord of the Universe, though One, manifests Himself differently according to the different likings of His worshipers, and each one of them has his own view of God which he values most. To some He is a kind master or a loving father, a sweet smiling mother or a devoted friend, and to others a faithful husband or a dutiful and obliging son.

—*Sri Ramakrishna*

Adore God as thou wouldst if Thou sawest Him; for, if thou seest Him not, He seeth thee.

—*Prophet Mohammad*

He who, dwelling in all things,
Yet is other than all things,
Whom all things do not know,
Whose body all things are,
Who controls all things from within—
He is your Soul, the Inner Controller,
The Immortal.

J. Needham

God is the symphony of mind, the wordless Harmony; God is the embodiment of all learning, and He is immanent in all His creation.

—*Japji*

Man has to worship God in the form of man. God appears before him as a blind beggar, an idiot, a leper, a child, a decrepit old man, a criminal or a mad man. You must see, even behind these veils, the Divine Embodiment of Love, Power and Wisdom, the *Sai*, and worship Him through *seva* or service.

—*Sathya Sai Baba*

All Things Bright and Beautiful

All things bright and beautiful,
　All creatures great and small,
All things wise and wonderful,
　The Lord God made them all.

Each little flower that opens,
　Each little bird that sings,
He made their glowing colours
　He made their tiny wings.

The purple-headed mountain,
　The river running by,
The sunset, and the morning
　That brightens up the sky,

The cold wind in the winter,
　The pleasant summer sun,
The ripe fruits in the garden,
　He made them every one.

The tall trees in the greenwood,
　The meadows where we play,
The rushes by the water,
　We gather every day.

He gave us eyes to see them,
　And lips that we might tell
How great is God Almighty,
　Who has made all things well.

—*Cecil Frances Alexander*

God, being cosmic vibration, is the Word. God, as the Word, is humming through all atoms. There is a music coming out of the universe that deeply meditating devotees can hear. Now at this moment, I am hearing His voice. The Cosmic Sound that you hear in meditation is the voice of God. That sound forms itself into a language intelligible to you. When I listen to *Aum* and occasionally ask God to tell me something, that sound of *Aum* changes into English or Bengali and gives me precise instructions.

—*Sri Sri Paramhansa Yogananda*

That which is beyond all beyonds is Supreme Light, is God. He is only in the heart. He is not outside.

—*Swami Muktanande*

Man is an infinite circle whose circumference is nowhere, but the centre is located in a spot; and God is an infinite circle whose circumference is nowhere, but whose centre is everywhere.
The highest concept we can have of God is man.
God Himself is your image.

—*Swami Vivekananda*

Thou art the marvellous magician, He who trans figures everything, makes beauty emerge out of ugliness, light out of darkness, clear water out of mud, knowledge out of ignorance, and kindness out of egoism.

—*The Mother*

I believe that God is here, and that we are as near Him now as ever we shall be: I do not believe He started this world agoing and went away and left it to run itself.

—*Hubbard*

Where art Thou, Lord?

The parish priest of austerity
    Climbed up in a high church steeple
To be nearer God so that He might hand
    His word down to His people.
When the sun was high, when the sun was low,
    The good man sat unheeding
Sublunary things from transcendency
    Was he forever reading
And now and again when he heard the creak
    Of the weather vane a-turning,
He closed his eyes, and said, "Of a truth.
    From God I am now learning".
And in sermon script he daily wrote
    What he thought was sent from heaven,
And he dropped this down on his peoples' heads
    Two times one day in seven.
In his age God said, "Come down and die!"
    And he cried out from the steeple,
"Where art Thou, Lord ?" And the Lord replied,
    "Down here among My people."

              —*William Crosswell Doane*

God and soul are the only realities—infintely more real than the world.

              —*Vivekananda*

In Him was life; and the life was the light of men. And the light shineth in darkness; and the darkness comprehendeth it not.

              —*Gospel of St. John*

If there should rise suddenly within the skies
Sunburst of a thousand suns
Flooding the earth with beams undeemed of,
Then might be that Holy One's
Majesty land radiance dreamed of.

—*Bhagavad Gita*

He forgets nothing, but forgives all.

—*Unknown*

You see many stars in the sky at night, but not when the sun rises. Can you, therefore, say that there are no stars in the heavens during the day? O man, because you cannot find God in the days of your ignorance, say not that there is no God.

—*Sri Ramakrishna*

Fire itself has no definite shape, but as glowing embers it assumes different forms. Thus, the formless form is seen endowed with forms. Similarly, the formless God sometimes invests Himself with definite forms.

—*Sri Ramakrishna*

For what is God? He is the soul of the universe.

—*Seneca*

He plays in every atom; He is playing when He is building up earths, and suns, and moons; He is playing with the human heart, the animals, the plants.

—*Swami Vivekananda*

God's Ways are Strange

God's ways are strange; He chastens those
   He loves, and gives them more of pain
   Than joy—and bids their hearts refrain
   From hatred of their darkest foes.

Yet we of Earth would not impose
   On those we love a galling chain—
   God's ways are strange.

And I have wondered that He chose
   Such trying means with which to gain
   A lasting good; but why complain
   Of thorns ? Enough to have the rose—
   God's ways are strange.

—Unknown

Who can sing His power? Who has the power to sing it.
Who can sing His gifts or know His signs?
Who can sing his attributes, His greatness and His deeds?
Who can sing His knowledge whose study is arduous?
Who can sing Him, who fashioneth the body and again destroyeth it?

In one salutation to thee, my God, let all my senses spread out and touch this world at thy feet. Like a flock of homesick cranes flying night and day back to their mountain nests, let all my life take its voyage to its eternal home in one salutation to thee.

—Rabindranath Tagore

I Think God is Proud

I think God is proud of those who bear
   A sorrow bravely—proud, indeed of them
Who walk straight through the dark to find Him there,
   And kneel in Faith to touch His garment's hem.
Oh, proud of them who lift their heads to shake.
   Among the tears from eyes that have grown dim,
Who tighten quivering lips and turn to take
   The only road they know that leads to Him.

How proud He must be of them—He who knows
   All sorrow, and how hard grief is to bear !
I think He sees them coming, and He goes
   With outstretched arms and hands to meet them
   there,
And with a look, a touch on hand or head,
   Each finds his hurt heart strangely comforted.
                    —*Grace Noll Crowell*

He, who is called *Brahma* or the *Most High*; who is the *Supreme Spirit* who permeates the whole universe; who is a true personification of existence, consciousness, and bliss; whose nature, attributes, and characteristics are holy; who is Omniscient, Infinite, Just and Merciful, who is the Author of the Universe, sustains and dissolves it; who awards all souls the fruits of their deeds in strict accordance with the requirements of absolute justice and is possessed of the like attributes, Him I believe to be the Great God.
                    —*Swami Dayananda Saraswati*

Who is supreme in heaven? Thou alone art supreme. Who is supreme on earth? Thou alone art supreme. Thy mighty word createth right and ordaineth justice for mankind, and thy powerful ordinance reacheth unto the uttermost parts of heaven and earth.

—Anonymous

One God—hidden in all creatures,
Pervading all, Inner Self of all things,
Surveying all deeds, abiding in all creatures,
Witness, Thinker, Alone, Unqualified.

—The Upanishads

I am the father of this world, the mother, the guardian, the father's father; I am the end of knowledge, the purifier, the sacred syllable, the hymn, the chant, the sacred sentence.

I am the ways, the supporter, the lord, the witness, the home, the refuge, the beloved; the forthcoming; and, withdrawing, the place, the treasure, the everlasting seed.

I am equal toward all beings; nor is any hatred or favoured of Me; but they who love Me with dear love, they are in Me and I in them.

—The Bhagavad Gita

God is day and night, winter and summer, and peace and war, satiety and hunger; but He takes various shapes; just as fire, when it is mingled with different incenses, is named according to the savour of each.

—Heraclitus

One Being and One
They call him *Indra, Mitra, Varuna* and *Agni*. To what is One, the poets give many a name.

—The Rig-Veda

20

But what things doest thou know
Looking Godward, to cry
'I am I, thou are thou,
I am low, thou art high?
I am thou, who thou seekest to find him;
find thou but thyself,
thou art I'
                              —*Algernon Charles Swinburne*

He is the first and the last; the seen and hidden; and He knoweth all things.
                              —*The Qur'an*

God is himself in no interval, nor extension of place, but in his immutable, pre-eminent all-possiblility that He is within everything, because all things are in Him, and without everything because he transcends all things.
                              —*Saint Augustine*

Our Lord God is an endless being without changing, almighty without failing, sovereign wisdom, light, soothness without error or darkness; sovereign goodness, love, peace, and sweetness.
                              —*Walter Hilton*

You are the dark blue butterfly,
You are the green parrot with red eyes,
You are the thunder-cloud, the seasons, the seas,
You are without beginning,
You pervade all things,
And from you all beings were born.
                              —*The Upanishads*

The Eternal Spring, whence streaming bounty flows!
The Eternal Light, whence every radiance glows!
The Eternal Height of indetermin'd space!
The Eternal Depth of condescending grace!
Supreme! and Midst! and Principal! and End!
The Eternal Father!. and the Eternal Friend!
The Eternal Love! who bounds in ev'ry breast;
The Eternal Bliss!. whence ev'ry creature's bless'd.

—*Henry Brooke*

God is light that is never darkened, an unwearied life that cannot die; a fountain always flowing; a garden of life; a seminary of wisdom; a radical beginning of all goodness.

—*Francis Quarles*

I am Alpha and Omega, the beginning and the end, the first and the last.

—*The New Testment Revelation*

The seed of all born beings likewise am I, O Arjun; there is naught that can be in existence, moving or unmoving, without Me.

—*The Bhagavad Gita*

Since the nature of the One produces all things, it is none of them. It is not a thing or quality or quantity or intellect or soul; It is not in motion or at rest, in place or in time, but exists in Itself, a unique Form; or rather It is formless, existing before all form, before motion, before rest; for these belong to being and make it multiple.

—*Plotinus*

All who have any education know that God has no right hand nor left; that he is not moved nor at rest, nor in a particular place, but that He is absolutely infinite and contains in Himself all perfections.

—*Benedict Spinoza*

By the nature of God I understand a Substance infinite, independent, all-knowing, all-powerful, and by which I myself and every other thing that exits were created.

—*Rene Descartes*

There is underlying all change a living Power that is change-less, that holds all together. That informing Power or Spirit is God. He alone is. This power is purely benevolent. God is life, Truth, Light. He is love. He is the Supreme Good.

—*Mohandas K. Gandhi*

The Creator took thought and discerned that, out of the things that are by nature visible, no work destitute of reason could be made so fair as that which possessed reason. He also saw that reason could not dwell in anything devoid of Soul. This being His thought He put Spirit in Soul and Soul in Body, that He might be the maker of the fairest and best of works. Hence we shall probably be safe in affirming that the universe is a living creature endowed with Soul and Spirit by the providence of God.

—*Plato*

But what is God? The universal Intelligence. What is God? did I say? All that you see and all that you cannot see. His greatness exceeds the bounds of thought. He is all in all, He is at once within and without His works. In us the better part is spirit, in Him there is nothing but spirit.

—*Lucius Annaeus Seneca*

Immortal!. Ages past, yet nothing gone!
Morn without eve! A race without a goal!
Unshorten'd by Progression infinite!
Futurity forever future! Life
beginning still, where computation ends!
'T is the description of a Deity!

—*Aristotle*

23

The Being who, to me, is the real God is the one who created the majestic universe and rules it. He is the only originator, the only originator of thoughts; thoughts suggested from within, not from without. The originator of colors and all their possible combinations; of forces and the laws that govern them; of forms and shapes of all the forms—man has never invented a new one. He is the only originator. He made the materials of all things; he made the laws by which, and by which alone, man may combine them into the machines. Something is missing? He made character—man can portray it but not create it, for He is the only creator. He is the perfect artisan, the perfect artist.

—*Edward Young*

God is mightiest in power, fairest in beauty, immortal in existence, supreme in virtue; therefore, being invisible to a mortal nature, He is seen through His works themselves.

—*Mark Twain*

God's deity is no prison in which he can exist only in and for Himself. It is rather his freedom to be in and for Himself but also with and for us, to assert but also to sacrifice Himself, to wholly exalted but also comepletely humble, not only almighty but almighty mercy, not only Lord but servant, not only judge but also Himself the judged, not only man's eternal King but also his brother in time. And all that, without in the slightest forfeiting his deity!

—*Karl Barth*

The world in all its detail, from the mechanical movement of what we call the atom of matter to the free-movement of thought in the human-ego, is the self-revelation of the "Great I am".

—*Mahomed Iqbal*

It is unseen, unrelated, inconceivable, unferable, unimaginable indescribable. It is the essence of the one self-cognition common to all states of consciousness. All phenomena cease in it. It is peace, it is bliss, it is nonduality.

—*The Upanishads*

Than whom there is naught else higher, than whom there is naught smaller, naught greater, One stands like a tree established in heaven; by him, the Person, is the whole universe filled.

—*The Upanishads*

All speculation concerning the mysteries of God is a very dangerous thing by which the willing spirit can be trapped. As long as the willing spirit follows the Spirit of God, it has strengths in its resigned humility to see all the wonders of God.

—*The Way to Christ*

Hail unto Thee, O Tranquil Soul!
Yea, hail to Thee, most hidden One!
Unthinkable, unlimited, beginningless and endless too!

—*The Upanishads*

I have no friend like God
Who gave me soul and body, and infused into me understanding.
He cherisheth and watcheth over all creatures;
He is wise and knoweth the secret of hearts.
The Guru is like a lake; we are his beloved swans;
In the water are many jewels and rubies.
God's praises are pearls, gems, and diamonds; singing them maketh soul and body happy!

—*The Adi Granth*

To Thee all things offer praise:
Day and night, lightnings, snows,
The heavens and the other, roots and growing things,
Beasts and birds and shoals of swimming fish.
                              —*Synesius of Cyrene Hymn*

DEVOTION

Love all God's creation, the whole and every grain of sand in it. Love every leaf, every ray of God's light. Love the animals, love the plants, love everything. If you love everything, you will perceive the divine mystery in things. Once you perceive it, you will begin to comprehend it better every day. And you will come at last to love the whole world with an all embracing love.

—Fyodor Dostoyevsky

Cling thou to Me!
Clasp Me with heart and mind! so shalt thou dwell
Surely with Me on high. But if thy thought
Droops from such height; if thou be'st weak to set
Body and soul upon Me constantly
Despair not! give Me lower service! seek
To reach Me, worshipping with steadfast will;
And if thou canst not worship steadfastly,
Work for Me, toil in works, pleasing to Me!
For he that laboureth right for love of Me
Shall finally attain! But, if in this
Thy faint heart fails, bring Me thy failure!

—Bhagavad Gita

O Lord, Thou knowest what is best for us, let this or that be done, as Thou shalt please. Give what Thou wilt, and how much Thou wilt, and when Thou wilt. Deal with me as Thou thinkest good, and as best pleaseth Thee. Set me where Thou wilt, and deal with me in all things just as Thou wilt. Behold, I am Thy servant, prepared for all things; for I desire not to live unto myself, but unto Thee; and Oh, that I could do it worthily and perfectly! AMEN.

—Thomas A. Kempis

Nay! but once more
Take My last word, My utmost meaning have!
Precious thou art to Me; right well beloved!
Listen! I tell thee for thy comfort this.
Give Me thy heart! adore Me! serve Me! cling
In faith and love and reverence to Me!
So shalt thou come to Me! I promise true,
For thou art sweet to Me!
    And let go those—
Rites and writ duties! Fly to me alone!
Make Me thy single refuge! I will free
Thy soul from all its sins! Be of good cheer!

—Bhagavad Gita

If a man say, I love God, and hateth his brother, he is a liar: for he that loveth not his brother whom he hath seen, how can he love God whom he hath not seen?

And this commandment have we from him, that he who loveth God loveth his brother also.

—New Testament

Live in God

Live in God before you blame your luck
Whatever you think, will make your luck.
Have faith in Him and selfless service
Follow the path of truth, and think no evil.
Entertain God alone.
The reward of worship is not prosperity.
Such is not a thing of the spirit.
You may or may not get success.
For it mostly depends upon effort.
But one thing is certain: *You will have*
When you live in God and obey His law
Peace, Happiness and Self-control.

—Unknown

If we work upon marble, it with perish; if upon brass, time will efface it; if we rear temples, they will crumble into dust; but if we work upon our immortal minds—if we imbue them with principles, with the just fear of God and love of followmen—we engrave on those tablets something which will brighten through all eternity.

—Daniel Webster

For everything there is an appropriate way of polishing; the heart's polishing is the remembrance of God.

—Hadith of Tirmidhi

All you who come before me, hoping to attain the accomplisment of your desires, pray with hearts pure from falsehood, clean within and without, reflecting the truth like a mirror.

—*Oracle of Temmangu*

And Jesus said unto him: Thou shalt Love the Lord thy God with all thy heart, and with all thy soul, and with all thy mind. This is the first and great commandment.

And the second is like unto it: Thou shalt love thy neighbour as thyself. On these two commandments hang all the laws and the prophets.

—*The New Testament*

The Lord is nigh to all who call upon him—to all who call upon him in truth.

—*Bible*

They that wait upon the Lord shall renew their strength,
They shall run and not be weary;
They shall walk and not faint.

—*Isaiah*

Filth on hands, feet, and body may be washed off with water; clothes fouled by dirt may be washed with soap; the mind fouled by sin and evil may only be cleansed by devotion to God.

—*Adi Granth Japji*

One should chant the holy name of the Lord in a humble state of mind, thinking oneself lower than the straw in the street; one should be more tolerant than a tree, devoid of all sense of false prestige, and should be ready to offer all respects to others. In such a state of mind one can chant the holy name of the Lord constantly.

—*Sikshashtakam*

The intellects of those who lack fixity of spiritual purpose are inconsistent, their interests endlessly ramified.

—Bhagavad Gita

Love, indeed, is light from heaven
A spark of that immortal fire
With angels shared, by Allah given
To lift from earth our low desire
Devotion wafts the mind above,
But Heaven itself descends in love;
A feeling from the Godhead caught;
To wean from self each sordid thought;
A ray of Him who form'd the whole;
A glory circling round the soul.

—Byron

For whosoever will save his life shall lose it; and whosoever will lose his life for my sake shall find it.

—The New Testament

I am the way, the truth, and the life

—The New Testament

My son, do not despise the
   Lord's discipline
Or be weary of his reproof.
For the Lord reproves him
   Whom he loves.
As a father the son in
Whom he delights.

—Proverbs

To the eyes of men athirst the whole world seems in dream as a spring of water.

—Saadi

To look on high, to learn what is beyond, to seek to raise oneself always.

—Socrates

God is Love

Many are the means described for the attainment of the highest good, such as love, performance of duty, self-control, truthfulness, sacrifices, gifts, austerity, charity, vows, observance of moral percepts. I could name more. But of all I could name verily love is the highest: love and devotion that make one forgetful of everything else, love that unites the lover with me. What ineffable joy does one find through love of me, the blissful Self! Once that joy is realised, all earthly pleasures fade into nothingness.

—*Srimad Bhagavatam*

In the same way that the mind seeks variety in foods and other things, so does it want diversity in *sadhana*. It rebels against monotonous practices... To cease *sadhana* is a grave error. The practice must never be renounced under any circumstances. Bad thoughts will always be pressing to penetrate into the mental laboratory; if the aspirant suspends his *sadhana* his mind becomes the workshop of Satan.

Swami Sivananda

There can be but one universal creed for man—that is loyalty to God. It includes, when it is not inconsistent, loyalty to king, country, and humanity. But it equally often excludes all these.

—*Mahatma Gandhi*

To those who are ever attached to Me, and who worship me with love, I impart discernment, by means of which they attain Me. Out of My love for them, I, the Divine within them, set alight in them the radiant lamp of wisdom, thereby dispelling the darkness of their ignorance.

—*Bhagavad Gita*

Though a man be soiled with the sins of a liftime,
Let him but love me, rightly resolved, in utter devotion:
I see no sinner; that man is holy.

—The Bhagavad Gita

If you fear God, cast yourself into His arms, and then His hands cannot strike you.

—Saint Augustine Sermons

Whatever a man offers to Me, whether it be a leaf, or a flower, or fruit, or water, I accept it, for it is offered with devotion and purity of mind.

—The Bhagavad Gita

FAITH

*—Faith is not belief; it is the grasp of
the Ultimate — an illumination.
He who has no faith in himself can
never have faith in God.*
    —Swami Vivekananda

Ah! ye who into this ill world are come—
Fleeting and false—set your faith fast on Me!
Fix heart and thought on Me! Adore Me!
Bring offerings to Me! Make Me prostrations!
Make Me your supremest joy! and, undivided,
Unto My rest your spirits shall be guided.

—*Bhagavad Gita*

Ask, and it shall be given you; seek, and ye shall find; knock,
and it shall be opened unto you...
Verily I say unto you. If ye have faith, and doubt not... if ye
shall say unto this mountain, be thou removed, and be thou
cast into the sea; it shall be done.
And all things, whatsoever ye shall ask in prayer, believing,
ye shall receive.

—*Gospel of St. Mathew*

Our honesty and upright conduct
Are not mere matters of policy
Or convenience : all our life in this world
Must be lived as in the presence of God.
The finest example of faith we have
In the Apostle's life: full of faith,
Let us render willing obedience
To God's Will. Our responsibility,
Though great, is not a burden
Greater than we can bear: let us
Pray for God's assistance, and He will help.

—*Qur'an*

Then was Jesus led up of the spirit into the wilderness to be tempted of the devil.

And when he had fasted forty days and forty nights, he was afterward an hungred.

And when the tempter came to him, he said, If thou be the Son of God, command that these stones be made bread.

But he answered and said, It is written, Man shall not live by bread alone, but by every word that proceedeth out of the mouth of God.

Then the devil taketh him up into the holy city, and setteth him on a pinnacle of the temple,

And saith unto him, If thou be the Son of God, cast thyself down: for it is written, He shall give his angels charge concerning thee: and in their hands they shall bear thee up, lest at any time thou dash thy foot against a stone.

Jesus said unto him, It is written again. Thou shalt not tempt the Lord thy God.

Again, the devil taketh him up into an exceeding high mountain, and sheweth him all the kingdoms of the world, and the glory of them;

And saith unto him, All these things will I give thee, if thou with fall down and worship me.

Then saith Jesus unto him, Get thee hence, Satan: for it is written, Thou shalt worship the Lord thy God, and him only shalt thou serve.

Then the devil leaveth him, and behold, angels came and ministered unto him.

—*Gospel of St. Mathew*

Arjuna: What is the fate of him who strives with faith,
But fails, and loses heart; or even falls
From holiness, missing the perfect rule?
Like the rent cloud that quickly vanishes,
Is he not lost, abandoning the Way?
Remove, O Krishna, my uncertainties!
No one but Thou canst banish my grave doubts.

Krishna: Arjuna, none who works for self-redemption
Will ever meet an evil destiny!
Not here on earth, nor in the other world
Will he encounter sorrow and destruction.

A fallen yogi, when he dies, attains
The heavenly regions of the virtuous!
Many the years he dwells there, joyfully.
And when at last he must return to earth,
His past true deeds will cause him to take birth
In some pure, noble-minded family,
Happy in virtue and prosperity.

Even it may be that he will take birth
Into the home of *yogis*, calm and wise:
Enlightened souls ! Ah, but this kind of birth
Is all too rarely come by here on earth!

Returning here, his good deeds of the past
Awaken in his heart the urge to seek
His former path with ever greater zeal,
Determined more than ever, now, to reach
The one true goal of life: Eternal Bliss.

Past *yoga* practice, like an unseen tide,
Propels him forcefully upon his Way.
Even that man who deeply longs to know
The subtle *yoga* path is more advanced
Than those who merely practise outward rites,
Or follow Scripture for their private gain.

By diligently purging self of sin
(An end achieved at last by all who strive),
The *yogi*, countless rebirths endeed, dwells
Forever in Supreme Beatitude!

Greater the *yogi* is than they who quell
Their senses with ascetic discipline:
Greater than they who seek to plumb the depths
Of truth by reasoning and wise dispute:
Greater than they who seek by works alone
To impress the Lord, who is Himself those works!
Be thou therefore a *yogi*, O Arjuna!
He who absorbs his mind and soul in Me,
Unceasingly established in My rest,
Known him to be, among all *yogis*, best.

—*Bhagavad Gita*

The Great News for man, in his spiritual Destiny,
Is the Judgment to come, the Day of Sorting Out.
Do not the Power, the Goodness, and the Justice
Of God reveal themselves in all nature?—
The Panorama around us, the voice in our souls,
And the harmony between heaven and earth?
That Day is sure to arrive at its time
Appointed, when behold! the present order
Will pass away. Then will the Fruits
Of Evil appear, and the Fruits of Righteousness
God's blessings will be more than the merits of men;
But who can argue with the Fountain of Grace?
And who can prevent the course of Justice?
Let us then, before it becomes too late,
Betake ourselves to our Lord Most Gracious!

—*Qur'an*

Therefore I say unto you: What things soever ye desire, when
ye pray, believe that ye receive them, and ye shall have them.

—*The New Testament*

I am the vine, ye are the branches: He that abideth in me, and I in him, the same bringeth forth much fruit: for without me ye can do nothing.

If a man abide not in me, he is cast forth as a branch, and is withered; and men gather them, and cast them into the fire, and they are burned.

If ye abide in me, and my words abide in you, ye shall ask what ye will, and it shall be done unto you.

Herein is my Father glorified, that ye bear much fruit; so shall ye be my disciples.

—*Gospel of St. John*

Faith is the limitless power of God within you. God knows through His consciousness that He created everything; so faith means the knowledge and conviction that we are made in the image of God. When we are attuned to His consciousness within us, we can create worlds. Remember, in your will lies the almighty power of God. When a host of difficulties comes and you refuse to give up in spite of them; when your mind becomes 'set', then you will find God responding to you.

—*Sri Sri Paramhansa Yogananda*

Though I wall through the valley of the shadow of death,
I will fear no evil: for thou art with me;
Thy rod and thy staff, they comfort me.

—*Bible*

The sun, with all its planets moving around it, can ripen the smallest bunch of grapes as if it had nothing else to do. Why then should I doubt His power?

—*Galileo*

Never are we nearer the Light than when the darkness is deepest.

—*Swami Vivekananda*

39

If but one message I may leave behind,
One single word of courage for my kind,
It would be this – Oh, brother, sister, friend,
Whatever life may bring – What God may send,
No matter whether clouds lift soon or late—
Take heart and wait

Despair may tangle darkly at your feet,
Your faith be dimmed, and hope, once cool and sweet,
Be lost–but suddenly, above a hill
A heavenly lamp, set on a heavenly sill,
Will shine for you and point the way to go,
How well I know!

For I have wanted through the dark, and I
Have seen a star rise in the blackest sky.
Repeatedly–it has not failed me yet;
And I have learned God will never forget
To light the lamp—if we but wait for it
It will be lit.

—*Grace Crowell*

The Blind Man

I see a blind man every day
Go bravely down the street
He walks as if the path were clear
Before his steady feet.
Save when he fumbles with his cane,
I almost feel he sees
The passers by who smile at him,
The flowers and the trees

He comes to corners where the crowd
Of traffic suits about,
But when he hesitates, some hand

40

Will always help him out.
He crosses pavements fearlessly –
It is as if he knows
That there are unknown, watchful friends
Along the way he goes!

Sometimes we walk through unseen paths,
Sometimes the road ahead
Is shrouded in the mists of fear;
But we are being led
As surely as the blind man is...
And we seem to sway,
A hand will find us in the dark
And guide us on our way.

—*Margaret Sangster*

A firm faith in God is the only ray of hope that penetrates the gloom of fear and ignorance.

—*Rig Veda*

The one who has faith and trust in the Lord invariably conquers adverse circumstances and emerges the winner, rich with bounty in the struggle of life.

—*Rig Veda*

They that know Thy name will put their trust in Thee: for Thou, Lord, hast not forsaken them that seek Thee.

—*The Old Testament*

All men deserve to be saved, but he above all deserves immortality who desires it passionately, even in the face of reason.

—*Miguel De Unamuno*

The Doubter

"Show me your God !" the doubter cries
I point him to the smiling skies;
I show him all the woodland greens;
I show him peaceful sylvan scenes;
I show him winter snows and frost;
I show him waters tempest-tossed;
I show him hills, rock-ribbed and strong;
I bid him hear the thrush's song;
I show him flowers in the close
The lily, violet and the rose;
I show him rivers, babbling streams;
I show him youthful hopes and dreams;
I show him maids with eager hearts;
I show him toilers in the marts;
I show him stars, the moon, the sun;
I show him the deeds of kindness done;
I show him joy; I show him care,
And still he holds his doubting air,
And faithless goes his way, for he
Is blind of soul; and cannot see.

—*John K. Bangs*

One ship drives East and another drives West with the
    selfsome winds that blow.
'Tis the set of the sails—and not the gales
    Which tells us the way to go.
Like the winds of the sea are the ways of fate,
    As we voyage along through life;
'Tis the set of a soul that decides its goal,
    And not the calm or the strife.

—*Ella Wheeler Wilcox*

The Rainy Day

The day is cold, and dark, and dreary;
It rains and the mind is never weary;
The vine still clings to the moldering wall,
But at every gust the dead leaves fall
And the day is dark and dreary
My life is cold, and dark, and dreary;

It rains and the mind is never weary;
My thoughts still cling to the mouldering past,
But the hopes of youth fall thick in the blast,
And the day is dark and dreary
Be still, sad heart ! and cease repining;
Behind the clouds is the sun still shining;
Thy fate is the common fate of all,
Into each life some rain must fall,
Some days must be dark and dreary
                    —*Henry Wadsworth Longfellow*

A Hymn of Trust

O love divine, that stooped to share
Our sharpest pang, our bitterest tear!
On thee we cast each earth-born care;
We smile at pain while thou art near.

Though long the weary way we tread,
And sorrow crown each lingering year,
No path we shun, no darkness dread,
Our hearts still whispering, thou art near.

43

When drooping pleasure turns to grief,
And trembling faith is changed to fear,
The murmuring mind, the quivering leaf,
Shall softly tell us, thou art near.

On thee we rest out burdening woe,
O Love divine, for ever dear!
Content to suffer while we know,
Living and dying, thou art near.

—Oliver Wendell Holmes

Faith in My Life

I choose for my subject faith wrought into life, apart from creed or dogma. By faith I mean a vision of good one cherishes and the enthusiasm that pushes one to seek its fulfilment regardless of obstacles. Faith is a dynamic power that breaks the chain of routine and gives a new, fine turn to old commonplaces. Faith reinvigorates the will, enriches the affection and awakens a sense of creativeness.

Trust in my fellowmen, wonder at their fundamental goodness and confidence that after this night of sorrow and oppression they will rise up strong and beautiful in the glory of morning. Reverence for the beauty and preciousness of earth, and a sense of responsibility to do what I can to make it a habitation of health and plenty for all men.

Even if my vital spark should be blown out, I believe that I should behave with courageous dignity in the presence of fate and strive to be a worthy companion of the Beautiful, the Good and the True. But fate has its master in the faith of those who surmount it, and limitation has its limits for those who, though disillusioned, live greatly. True faith is not a fruit of security, it is the ability to blend mortal fragility with the inner strength of the spirit. It does not shift with the changing shade of one's thought.

Helen Keller

44

I believe that we should not forget how to disagree agreeably
and how to criticise constructively. I believe with all my heart
that we must not become a nation of mental mutes blindly
following demagogues.

I believe that in our constant search for security we can
never gain any peace of mind until we secure our own soul.
And this I do believe above all, especially in my times of
greater discouragement, that I must believe, that I must
believe in my fellowmen—that I must believe in myself—that
I must believe in God—if life is to have any meaning.

—*Margaret Chase Smith*

Do not give way. Hold tight. It is when everything seems lost
that all is saved.

—*The Mother*

There is no Unbelief

There is no unbelief;
Whoever paints a seed beneath the sod
And waits to see it push away the clod
   He trusts in God.
  There is no unbelief;
Whoever says beneath the sky,
"Be patient, heart; light breaketh by and by,"
   Trusts the Most High.

There is no unbelief;
Whoever sees' neath winter's field of snow,
The silent harvest of the future grow—
   God's power must know.
  There is no unbelief;
Whoever his down on his couch to sleep,
Content to lock each sense in slumber deep,
   Knows God will keep.

There is no unbelief;
Whoever says "tomorrow", "the unknown",
"The future", trusts that power alone
  He dares disown.
There is no unbelief;
The heart that looks on when the eyelids close,
And dares to live when life has only woes,
  God's comfort knows.

There is no unbelief;
For this by day and night unconsciously
The heart lives by the faith the lips deny.
  God knoweth why.
                               —*Elizabeth York Case*

Amidst all the mysteries by which we are surrounded, nothing is more certain than that we are in the presence of an infinite and eternal energy from which all things proceed.
                                —*Herbert Spencer*

Good life and immortality are the rewards of the faithful. The religion of the Wise one will cleanse the faithful from all sin.
                                —*Zoroastrianism*

Faith is necessary for the virtuous life. One's faith will not be unrewarded. Prosperity follows upon Faith.
                                —*Buddhism*

Faith is necessary, but it must be accompanied by work. One who is faithful even to death, will receive a crown of life. He who asks in perfect faith shall receive. Faith is basic to all understanding.
                                —*Christianity*

He who lacks faith will not succeed. One must hold to faith at all times. Heaven makes great demands upon one's faith, but God is with man and he should never waver in the faith.

—*Confucianism*

Faith is the pathway to wisdom. This faith will come if one yearns in his heart for it. The most prized of God is the man of faith.

—*Hinduism*

The man of faith has chosen the right pathway. He should practise his faith at all times.

—*Jainism*

God is faithful and will preserve the faithful. The man of faith can expect great rewards from God.

—*Judaism*

Man should have faith in God for God will always prove faithful. But God has no patience with the unfaithful.

—*Mahammedanism*

Even the slightest yielding to doubt is a departing from the natural nature of man. Faith is fundamental to human beings.

—*Shintoism*

To have less than enough faith is to have no faith at all. The divine will repay faith with faith and faithlessness with faithlessness.

—*Tao Teh King*

Faith, hope and charity, those three virtues for whose building up is mounted all the scaffolding of the Bible, are only in the soul that believes what it sees not yet, and hopes and loves what it believes.

—*Saint Augustine*

Faith is an affirmation and an act
That bids eternal truth be fact.

—*Samuel Taylor Coleridge*

There is no unbelief;
And by day and night, unconsciously,
The heart lives by that faith the lips deny,
God knoweth why.

—*Edward Bulwer-Lytton*

The true conclusion is to turn our backs on apprehensions,
and embrace that shining and courageous virtue, Faith.
Hope is the boy, a blind, headlong, pleasant fellow; Faith is
the grave, experienced, yet smiling man. Hope looks for
unqualified success; but Faith counts certainty a failure, and
takes honourable defeat to be a form of victory.

—*Robert Louis Stevenson*

What faith in God needs to begin with is the fair and simple
assumption that great good can come to be, if we follow the
call of conscience toward the heights and reach out for all
possible resources in the struggle for good.

—*Walter Marshall Horton*

To stand in the darkness and yet know that God is light; to
want to know the truth about a thousand mysteries, the
answer to a thousand problems, and not find the truth, the
answers, anywhere, and yet to know beyond a peradventure
that God is not hiding from us anything which it is possible
and useful for us to know; to stand in the darkness and yet
know that God is light—that is a great and noble faith, a faith
to which no man can come who does not know God.

—*Phillips Brooks*

If faith is the pioneer that leads us to knowledge of persons and of moral possibilities; if by faith we discover ourselves, the outer world's existence and its unity, why should we be surprised that faith is our road to God?

—*Harry Emerson Fosdick*

If a man repeats God's name, his body, mind, and everything become pure. Why should one talk only about sin and hell and such things? Say but once, "O Lord, I have undoubtedly done wicked things, but I won't repeat them." And have faith in His name.

—*Sri Ramakrishna*

"Fear of God" never means to the Jews that they ought to be afraid of God, but that, trembling, they ought to be aware of his incomprehensibility. The fear of God is the creaturely knowledge of the darkness to which none of our spiritual powers can reach, and out of which God reveals himself. Therefore, "the fear of God" is rightly called "the beginning of knowledge" (Psalms111:10).
It is the dark gate through which man must pass if he is to enter into the love of God.

—*Martin Buber*

I thank thee, O Lord,
because thine eyes watch over my soul;
Thou hast rescued me from the jealousy of
the interpreter of lies,
from the congregation of those who seek
smooth things.
Thou hast redeemed the soul of the poor.

—*The Dead Sea Scrolls*

I know that my Redeemer liveth,
Tough He be the last to arise upon earth!
For from within my skin, this has been marked,
And from my flesh do I see God.

—*The Old Testament*

Lperhaps this is the destined hour
When hell shall lose its fatal power
And heaven itself shall bend above
To hail the soul redeemed by love.

—*Emily Bronte*

Into the matrix of Life darkly divinely resumed,
Man and his littleness perish, erased like an error and cancelled,
Man and his greatness survive, lost in the greatness of God.

—*Sir William Watson*

Everything comes from God except the fear of God.

—*Basque Proverb*

DUTY (*KARMA*)

Oh, face to face with trouble,
Friend, I have often stood—
To learn that pain hath sweetness,
To know that God is good.
Arise and meet the day light,
Be strong and do yourbest,
With an honest heart and a
childlike trust That God will
do the rest.

—Margaret Songster

I Think God is Proud

I think God is proud of those who bear
A sorrow bravely—proud indeed of them
Who walk straight through the dark to find Him there,
And kneel in faith to touch his garment's hem.
Oh, proud of them who lift their heads to shake,
Away the tears from eyes that have grown dim,
Who tighten quivering lips and turn to take
The only road they know that leads to Him,

How proud He must be of them—He who knows
All sorrow, and how hard grief is to bear !
I think He sees them coming, and He goes
With outstretched arms and hands to meet them there,
And will a look, a touch an land or head,
Each finds his hurt heart strangely comforted.

—*Graee Noll Crowell*

To have striven, to have made any effort, to have been true
to certain ideals—this alone is worth the struggle. We are
here to add what we can to, not to get what we can from life.

—*Sir William Osler*

There is no flaw in this law of *Karma*. No reservation. It is an
exact and accurate regulation of actions and reactions. Man
eats what he cooks. That is, he reaps what he sows.

—*Athar Veda*

Improve of others not by reasoning but by example. Let your
existence, not your words, be your preaching.

—*Amiel*

A Prayer

Let me do my work each day;
And if the darkened hours of anxiety overcome me,
May I not forget the strength that comforted me
In the desolation of other times.
May I still remember the bright hours that found me
Walking over the silent hills of earlier days,
Or dreaming on the margin of the quiet river...
When I vowed to have courage
Amid the tempests of the changing years.
Spare me from bitterness
And from the sharp passions of unguarded moments.
May I not forget that poverty and true riches are of the spirit.
Though the world know me not,
May my thoughts and actions be such
As shall keep me friendly with myself...
Give me a few friends who will love me for what I am;
And keep ever burning before my vagrant steps
The kindly light of hope.
And though age and infirmity overtake me,
And I come not within sight of the castle of my dreams,
Teach me still to be thankful for life,
And for time's olden memories that are good and sweet;
And may the evening's twilight find me gentle still.

—Max Ehrmann

We live in deeds, not years; in thoughts, not breaths; in
feelings, not in figures on a dial. We should count time by
heart-throbs. He most lives who thinks most, feels the
noblest, acts the best.

—Bailey

The man who lives in the present, forgetful of the past and indifferent to the future, is the man of wisdom. The best preparation for tomorrow's work is to do your work as well as you can today. The best preparation for a life to come is to live now and here. Live right up to your highest and best.

—*Avebury*

To work alone thou hast the right, but never to the fruits thereof. Be thou neither actuated by the fruits of action, nor be thou attached to inaction. O Dhananjaya, abandoning attachment and regarding success and failure alike, be steadfast in *Yoga* and perform thy duties. Even-mindedness is called *Yoga*.

—*Bhagavad Gita*

Duty

I slept and dreamed that life was Beauty:
I woke and found that life was Duty:
Was then thy dream a shadowy life ?
Toil on, sad heart, courageously,
And thou shall find the dream to be
A noonday light and truth to thee.

—*Ellen Hooper*

Such a householder may be compared to a waterfowl. It is constantly diving under water; yet, by fluttering its wings only once, it shakes off all traces of wet......
One can live in the world after acquiring love of God. It is like breaking the jackfruit after rubbing your hands with oil: the sticky juice of the fruit will not smear them.

—*Sri Ramakrishna*

Every duty is holy, and devotion to duty is the highest form of worship of God; it is certainly a source of great help in enlightening and emanicipating the ignorance encumbered souls of the *Bhddhas*—the bound ones.

—Swami Vivekananda

The state of freedom from action [that is, of eternal rest in the spirit] cannot be achieved without action. No one, by mere renunciation and ourward non-involvement, can attain perfection.

—Bhagavad Gita

It is not possible for you to give up work altogether. Your very nature will lead you to it whether you like it or not. Therefore, the scriptures ask you to work in a detached spirit; that is to say, not crave for the work's results. To work in such a spirit of detachment is known as 'karma yoga'.

—Sri Ramakrishna

Life affords no higher pleasure than that of surmounting difficulties, passing from one step of success to another, forming new wishes, and seeing them gratified. He that labours in any great or laudable undertaking has his fatigues first supported by hope, and afterwards rewarded by joy.

—Samuel Johnson Longfellow

Before reaching the highest ideal, man's duty is to resist evil; let him work, let him fight, let him strike straight from the shoulder.

—Swami Vivekananda

Let then our first act every morning be to make the following resolves for the day: "I shall not fear anyone on earth. I shall fear only God. I shall not bear ill-will towards anyone. I shall conquer untruth by truth, and in resisting untruth I shall put up with all suffering."

—Mahatma Gandhi

In all I do or advise, the infallible test I apply is whether the particular action will hold good in regard to the dearest and the nearest. The teaching of the faith I hold dear is unmistakable and unequivocal in the matter. I must be the same to friend and foe.

—*Mahatma Gandhi*

Unaffected by outward joys and sorrows, or by praise and blame; secure in his divine nature; regarding with equal gaze a clod of mud, a stone, and a bar of gold; impartial toward all experiences, whether pleasant or unpleasant; firm-minded; untouched by either praise or blame; treating everyone alike whether friend or foe; free from the delusion that, in anything he does, he is the doer: Such an one has transcended Nature's triune qualities."

—*Bhagavad Gita*

The Tapestry Weaver

Let us take to our heart a lesson, no braver lesson can be,
From the ways of the tapestry weavers, on the other side of the sea.
Above their head the pattern hangs, they study it with care,
And as to and fro the shuttle leaps their eyes are fastened there.
They tell this curious thing besides, of the patient, plodding weaver;
He works on the wrong side evermore, but works for the right side ever.
It is only when the weaving stops, and the web is loosed and turned,
That he sees his real handiwork, that his marvelous skill is learned.
Ah, the sight of its delicate beauty ! It pays him for all its cost.

No rarer, daintier work than his was ever done by the frost !
Then the Master bringeth him golden hire and giveth him praise as well,
And now happy the heart of the weaver is, no tongue but his can tell
The year of man are the looms of God, let down from the place of the sun,
Wherein we all are weaving, till the mystic web is done,
Weaving blindly but weaving surely, each for himself his fate;
We may not see how the right side looks, we can only weave and wait.
But, looking above for the pattern, no weaver hath need to fear;
Only let him look clear into Heaven—the perfect Pattern is there.
If he keeps the face of the Saviour forever and always in sight,
His toil shall be sweeter than honey, and his weaving is sure to be right.
And when his task is ended, and the web is turned and shown,
He shall hear the voice of the Master; it shall say to him, "Well done !"
And the white-winged angels of heaven, to bear him thence shall come down,
And God shall give him gold for his hire—not coin, but a crown !

—*Anson G. Chester*

If all your acts toward others, and even your thoughts of others, are registered in your subconscious mind through the principle of auto-suggestion, thereby building your own character in exact duplicate of your thoughts and acts, can you not see how important it is to guard those acts and thoughts ?... Every act and every thought you release modifies your own character in exact conformity with the nature of the act or the thought, and your character is a sort of centre of magnetic attraction which attracts to you the people and conditions that harmonise with it.

You cannot indulge in an act toward another person without having first created the nature of that act in your own thought, and you cannot release a thought without planting the sum and substance and nature of it in your own subconscious mind—there to become a part and parcel of your own character.

—*Napoleon Hill*

I have acted, I have caused others to act, and I have approved of others' actions. One should first comprehend that all such actions taking place in the world are the cause of the influx of *karma* particles, and then should forswear them

—*Acarangasutra*

St. Augustine teaches us that there is in every man a serpent, an Eve and an Adam. The serpent is the senses and our nature, the Eve is the concupiscible appetite, and the Adam is the reason, Nature tempts us continually, concupiscible appetite often fills us with desires, but the sin is not consummated if reason does not consent. Let the serpent and the Eve therefore act if we cannot hinder it; but let us pray to God that His grace may so strengthen our Adam that he may remain victorious.

—*Blaise Pascal*

Do what thou knowest to be good without expecting from it any glory. Forget not that the vulgar are a bad judge of good actions.

—*Demophilus*

But the higher you raise yourself, the smaller you will seem to the eyes that are envious. He who ranges on the heights is the one whom men most detest.

—Firdausi

Apply thyself to think what is good, speak what is good, do what is good.

—Zend-Avesta

Arise and be not slothful! Follow the straight path! He who walks, lives happy in this world and in those beyond.

—Dhammapada

Be thou faithful unto death.

—Revelations

Show not respect in especial to those that are esteemed great and high in place, but treat with a like respect those that are judged to be small and at the bottom of the social ladder.

—Tolstoy

TRUTH–KNOWLEDGE

To see a world in a grain of sand
And a heaven in a wild flower,
Hold infinity in the palm of
   your hand,
And eternity in an hour.
                    —William Blake

What was the time, the date, the day,
The season and the month when the Universe was created?
Pandits did not discover that, otherwise they would have
written a scripture, *Purana*, on that.
Nor did any Muslim divine know the time, other wise he
would have written it in a commentary on the *Quran*.
Neither did the *Yogi* or other mortal know of the day, the
date, the season and the month of this creation.
Only the Creator Himself knows when He did create the
world.

—Japji

All things are everywhere by Nature wrought
In interaction of the qualities.
The fool, cheated by self, thinks, 'This I did'
And 'That I wrought'; but—ah, thou strong-armed prince! —
A better-lessoned mind, knowing the play
Of visible things within the world of sense,
And how the qualities must qualify,
Standeth aloof even from his acts.

—Bhagavad Gita

Why, all the Saints and Sages who discussed
Of the two Worlds so wisely—they are thrust
Like foolish Prophets forth; their Words to scorn
Are scattered, and their Mouths are stopped with Dust.

With them the Seed of Wisdom did I sow,
And with mine own hand wrought to make it grow;
And this is all the Harvest that I reaped—
"I come like Water, and like Wind I go".

I sent my Soul through the Invisible
Some letter of that After-life to spell:
And by and by my Soul returned to me,
And answered, "I Myself am Heaven and Hell".

—Omar Khayyam

Truth is within ourselves, it takes no rise
From outward things, whate'er you may believe.
There is an inmost centre in us all,
Where truth abides in fullness.

—*Robert Browning*

The Brotherhood of Truth is one in all ages:
It is narrow men who create sects.
Let them not think that the goods
Of this world can shield them from evil
Or its consequences. God's Truth and His Messenger
Can be known to all: for He in His Mercy
Has given us faculties and judgment, if we
Would but use them. The Message is not
New: All creation proclaims it: High
Above all is the Lord of Glory Supreme !

—*Qur'an*

God's Truth comes to man in revelation
And in nature. How noble are His works !
How sublime His government of the world !
They all declare forth His glory !
Yet man must strangely resist Faith,
And ask to see the Signs of His power
Rather than the Signs of His Mercy !
Doth not His knowledge search through
The most hidden things ? Are not
Lightning and Thunder the Signs of His Might
As well as of His Mercy ? He alone
Is Worthy of praise, and His Truth
Will stand when all vanities pass
Away like scum on the torrent of Time.

—*Qur'an*

How do we come to think of things rather than of processes in this absolute flux ? By shutting our eyes to the successive events. It is an artificial attitude that makes sections in the stream of change and calls them things... When we shall know the truth of things, we shall realise row absurd it is for us to worship isolated products of the incessant series of transformations as though they were eternal and real. Life is no thing or state of a thing, but a continuous movement or change.

—*S. Radhakrishnan*

A man passes for what he is worth. What he is engraves itself on his face, on his form, on his fortunes, in letters of light which all men may read but himself... If you would not be known to do anything, never do it. A man may play the fool in the drifts of a desert, but every grain of sand shall seem to see.

—*Ralph Waldo Emerson*

The kingdom of heaven is already in existence if we will have it; that perfection is already in man if he will see it.

—*Swami Vivekananda*

A foolish man proclaimeth his qualifications;
A wise man keepeth them secret within himself;
A straw floateth on the surface of water,
But a precious gem placed upon it sinketh.

Subhashita Ratna Nidhi,

Let your old age be child-like, and your childhood like old age; that is so that neither may your wisdom be with pride, nor your humility without wisdom.

St. Augustine

The magnetic needle always points towards the north, and hence it is that the sailing vessel does not lose her course. So long as the heart of man is directed towards God, he cannot be lost in the ocean of worldliness.

Sri Ramakrishna

I look behind and after
And find that all is right.
In my deepest sorrows
There is the Soul of light.

—*Swami Vivekananda*

Lordship in right and in fact belongs
To God Most Gracious. Whose Goodness
And Glory and Power are writ large
On all His Creation. The beauty and order
Of the Heavens above us proclaim Him.
Then who can reject His Call but those
In pitiful delusion? And who can fail
To accept, that truly knows himself
And the mighty Reality behind him?
The earth and the good things thereof are prepared
For man by his Gracious Lord, Who guards
Him from hourly dangers. Who sustains
The wonderful flight of the birds in mid-air?
Above, and below, and in mid-air can we see
His boundless Signs. We know that His Promise
Of the Hereafter is true. The spring and source
Of the goodness of things is in Him, and will
Appear triumphant when the Hour is established.

—*Qur'an*

Beware of false prophets, which come to you in sheep's clothing, but inwardly they are ravening wolves. Ye shall know them by their fruits.Do men gather grapes of thorns, or figs of thistles?

Even so every good tree bringeth forth good fruit; but a corrupt tree bringeth forth evil fruit.

A good tree cannot bring forth evil fruit, neither can a corrupt tree bring forth good fruit. Wherefore by their fruits ye shall know them.

—*Gospel of St. Mathew*

The sage who knows God has as little need for the Scriptures as one might have for a pond when the whole land is covered in flood.

—*Bhagavad Gita*

The Self is never born, nor does it perish. Once existing, it cannot ever cease to be. It is birthless, eternal, changeless, ever itself. It is not slain when the body is killed.

—*Bhagavad Gita*

Truth will preach itself; it will not die for the want of helping hands of me.
Truth is the fruit of realisation; therefore, seek it within the soul.
Truth is purity, truth is all knowledge; truth must be strengthening, must be enlightening, must be invigorating.
Every vision of Truth that man has is a vision of Him and of none else.

—*Swami Vivekananda*

God is even though the world deny Him. Truth stands, even though there be no public support. It is self-sustained. Truth is perhaps the most important name of God. In fact, it is more correct to say that Truth is God than to say that God is truth.

—*Mahatma Gandhi*

Abstract truth has no value, unless it incarnates in human beings who represent it by proving their readiness to die for it.

—*Mahatma Gandhi*

Kill therefore with the sword of wisdom the doubt born of ignorance that lies in thy heart. Be one in self-harmony, in *Yoga*, and arise, great warrior, arise.

—*Bhagavad Gita*

That which is the finest essence—this whole world has that as its soul. That is Reality. That is *Atman*. That art thou.

—*Chandogya Upanishod*

Remember, no human condition is ever permanent. Then you will not be overjoyed in good fortune nor too sorrowful in misfortune.

—*Socrates*

The mind from the beginning is of a pure nature, but since there is the finite aspect of it which is sullied by finite views, there is the sullied aspect of it. Although there is this defilement, yet the original pure nature is eternally unchanged. This mystery the Enlightened One alone understands.

—*Asvaghosha*

Praise the Lord from the earth; ye dragons, and all deeps; fire and hail; snow, and vapours; stormy wind fulfilling his word; mountains, and hills; fruitful trees, and tall cedars; beasts, and all cattle; creeping things and flying fowl; kings of the earth, and all people, princes, and all judges of the earth; both, youngmen and maidens; old men and children; let them praise the name of the Lord, for His name is excellent; His glory is above the earth and heaven.

—*Bible*

Ever this eternal light of Unity,
This mystic light of God's own Will,
Has shone and shines with undiminished splendour.
The names of many messengers are inscribed
In the records of many nations and many tongues,
And many were the forms in which their message was
delivered,
According to the needs of the times and the understanding
of the people;
And manifold were the lives of the Messangers,
And manifold also was the response of their people;
But they all witnessed to the One Truth:
Of God's unity, might, grace and love.

—*Qur'an*

To the enlightened man... whose consciousness embraces
the universe, to him the universe becomes his 'body' while
his physical body becomes a manifestation of the Universal
Mind, his inner vision an expression of the highest reality,
and his speech an expression of eternal truth.

Lama Anagarika Govinda

The great extension of our experience in recent years has
brought to light the insufficiency of our simple mechanical
conceptions and, as a consequence, has shaken the founda-
tion on which the customary interpretation of observation
was based.

Niels Bohr

All things in fact begin to change their nature and appearance;
one's whole experience of the world is radically different...
There is a new vast and deep way of experiencing, seeing,
knowing, contacting things.

Sri Aurobindo

For, in and out, about, above, below
'Tis nothing but a magic, shadow show.
Played in a box whose candle is the Sun,
Where we, moving figures, come and go.

—*Omar Khayyam*

O my brother ! A pure heart is as a mirror; cleanse it with the burnish of love and severance from all save God, that the true sun may shine within it and the eternal morning dawn.

—*Unknown*

Morality is not the blind following of a social impulse, but a habit of action based upon character—character moulded by that knowledge of truth which must become an integral part of our being.

—*Karl Pearson*

If Truth cannot save man, nothing can.

—*John Robertson*

The whole succession of men during the course of so many centuries should be considered as one Man, ever living and constantly learning.

—*Pascal*

Every man who returns into himself will find there traces of the Divinity.

—*Cicero*

The soul of man is the mirror of the world.

—*Leibnitz*

The soul is the image of what is above it and the model of what is below it. Therefore by knowing and analysing itself it knows all things without going out of its own nature.

—*Proclus*

The whole dignity of man is in thought. Labour then to think aright.

—*Pascal*

One must receive the Truth from wheresoever it may come.
—*Maimonides*

Examine all things and hold fast that which is good.
—*St. Paul*

When they tell thee that thou must not search everywhere for truth, believe them not. Those who speak thus are thy most formidable enemies—and Truth's.
—*Tolstoy*

Ignorance is the night of the spirit, but a night without stars or moon.
—*Chinese Proverb*

There is a stain worse than all stains, the stain of ignorance. Purify yourself of that stain, O disciples, and be free from soil.
—*Dhammapada*

Happy are they whom Truth herself instructs not by words and figures but by showing herself as she is.
—*Thomas A Kempis*

So long as one has not become as simple as a child one cannot expect the divine illumination. Forget all the knowledge of the world that you have acquired and become as ignorant as a child; then you shall attain to the divine wisdom.
—*Ramakrishna*

Love is greater than knowledge... because it is its own end.
—*Narada Sutra*

Love is an invisible, a sacred and ineffable spirit which traverses the whole world with its rapid thoughts.
—*Empedocles*

Beyond all other men make thyself the friend of him who is distinguished by his virtue. Yield always to his gentle warnings and observe his honourable and useful actions.

—Pythagoras

Be your own torch and your own refuge. Take truth for your force, take truth for your refuge. Seek refuge in no other but only in yourself.

—Mahaparinibbana Sutta

Prepare thyself for thou must travel alone. The Master can only indicate to thee the road.

—Golden Precepts

All the knowledge one can require emanates from this love.

—Antoine the Healer

He who walketh with the wise, shall be wise.

—Proverbs

Employ all the leisure you have in listening to the well-informed; so you shall learn without difficulty what they have learned by long labour.

—Isocrates

The soul not being mistress of itself, one looks but sees not, listens but hears not.

—Tseng Tse

A bad thought is the most dangerous of thieves.

—Chinese Buddhist Scriptures

It is far more useful to commune with oneslf than with others.

—Demophilus

70

My God is Manifest

I see in every tree that grows,
   In seed that all contains,
In every wind, and cloud that flows,
   In fertilizing rains,

In every stone whose atoms twirl,
   Yet seem so coldly still,
Or in the wood with living sap,
   Thy unresistless will.

In sands that at a vibrant sound
   Of music straight way leap,
And range themselves in beauteous forms
   From out of the inert heap.

In far-off stars, in blazing suns
   That never, never rest,
What tho' I cannot understand,
   My God is manifest.

No knowledge mine that when I die
   I e'er shall live again;
I am thy creature, and content
   With what thou dost ordain.

To thee I bow, I lift my soul,
   I, thy all-teeming clod,
Seen spirit—yet invisible—
   The Great, the Unknown God.

              —*Henrietta Huxley*

Nothing, not even the darkest falsehood, can stop the ultimate triumph of truth.

              —*The Mother*

He who beholds inaction in action, and action in inaction, is wise among men; he is one with the Spirit; he has attained the true goal of action (perfect freedom).

—Bhagavad Gita

True fear comes from faith; false fear comes from doubt. True fear is joined to hope, because it is born of faith, and because men hope in the God in whom they believe.

—Blaise Pascal Pensees

Where the Fearless One is, there is no fear of others. Where there is fear, there God is not.

—Kabir Hymns

All the aspects of the sea are not different from the sea; nor is there any difference between the universe and its supreme Principle.

—Chandogya Upanishad

It is the Spirit that is in men, it is the breath of the Almighty that gives them understanding.

—Job

Life is a journey in the darkness of the night.

—Panchatantra

The world is but a dream that passes and neither happiness nor sorrow are enduring.

—Firdausi

Everything is but a shadow cast by the mind.

—Ashwaghosha

It is not difficult to know the good, but is is difficult to put it in practice.

—Shu Ching

Intelligence divorced from virtue is no longer intelligence.

—*Minokhired*

Not superstitious rites but self-control allied to benevolence and beneficence towards all beings are in truth the rites one should accomplish in all places.

—*Ashoka*

One should maintain the vigour of the body in order to preserve that of the mind.

—*Vauvenargues*

For the tongue is a smouldering fire and abuse of speech a mortal poison; and while natural fire consumes bodies, the tongue consumes minds and hearts.

—*Baha-ullah*

Idleness like rust destroys much more than work uses up. A key in use is always clean.

—*Franklin*

Sincerity, a profound, grand, ingenuous sincerity is the first characteristic of all men who are in any way heroic.

—*Carlyle*

The man full of uprightness is happy here below, sweet is his sleep by night and by day his heart is radiant with peace.

—*Buddhist text*

All virtues are comprised in justice; if thou art just, thou art a man of virtue.

—*Theognis*

All the accidents of life can be turned to our profit.

—*Seneca*

Patience is sweeter than very honey, by this understand how useful it is to the soul that possesses it.

—*The Shepherd of Hermes*

To the persevering and the firm nothing is difficult.

—*Lun Yu*

He who was heedless and has become vigilant, shines over the darkened world like a moon in cloudless heavens.

—*Udanavagga*

Carelessness is not proper even for the worldling who derives vanity from his family and his riches; how much less for a disciple who has proposed to himself for his goal to discover the path fo liberation!

—*Fo-shu-hing-tsan-king*

It is only the coward who appeals always to destiny and never to courage.

—*Ramayana*

The saint does not seek to do great things; that is why he is able to accomplish them.

—*Lao Tse*

Personal success ought never to be considered the aim of existence.

—*Bacon*

It is good to have what one desires, but it is better to desire nothing more than what one has.

—*Menedemus*

Fear pleasure, it is the mother of grief.

—*Solon*

Our intelligence ought to govern us as a herdsman governs his goats, cows and sheep, preferring for himself and his herd all that is useful and agreeable.

—*Phio*

True strength is to have power over oneself.

—Tolstoy

The soul is its own witness, the soul is its own refuge. Never despise thy soul, that supreme witness in men.

—The Laws of Manu

The greatest man in the world is not the conqueror, but the man who has domination over his own being.

—Schopendaver

Blessed is he who keepeth himself pure.

—Quran

The wise weep not for the dead nor the living; all of us were before and shall not cease to be hereafter.

—Bhagavad Gita

Nothing is born of nothing, nothing can be annihilated, each commencement of being is only a transformation.

—Thales

Time takes away everything and gives everything; all changes but nothing is abolished, it is a thing immutable, eternal and always identical and one.

—Giordano Bruno

Only after having the experience of suffering have I learned the kinship of human souls to each other.

—Gogol

There can be no true freedom and happiness so long as men have not understood their oneness.

—Channing

Charity is the affection that impels us to sacrifice ourselves to humankind as if it were one being with us.

—Confucius

What is virtue? It is sensibility towards all creatures.

—*Hitopadesha*

He who is a friend of wisdom, must not be violent.

—*Fu-shu-hing-tsan-king*

Let no evil communication proceed out of your mouth, but that which is good that it may minister grace unto the hearers.

—*Ephasians*

The most perfect man is the one who is most useful to others.

—*Quran*

He has read everything, learned everything, practised everything, who has renounced his desires and lives without straining of hope.

—*Hitopadesha*

Eternity is for all time, but the world only for a moment. Sell not then for that moment thy kingdom of eternity.

—*Omar Khayyam*

They have gained this supreme perfection, to be totally masters of their thoughts.

—*Lotus Sutra*

To love long, unweariedly, always makes the weak strong.

—*Michelet*

All beings aspire to happiness, therefore envelop all in thy love.

—*Mahabharata*

Melt thy soul in the fire of love and thou wilt know that love is the alchemist of the soul.

—*Ahmed Halif*

The good man remains calm and serene.

—*Shih Ching*

MEDITATION

When your intellect, at present confused by the diversity of teaching in the Scriptures, becomes steadfast in the ecstacy of deep meditation, then you will achieve final union with God.
—Bhagavad Gita

A Better Man

In a world in which nuclear power exists man's only hope of survival is to be a better man. Up to this point in history man's greatest discoveries have been made in the realm outside of himself. He must now begin to explore more vigorously the "great within" of man—to discover the secrets of mind and spirit.

The discovery of nuclear power may do its greatest good by forcing us to change the direction of our thinking. Years before the discovery of nuclear power, Charles Proteus Steinmetz, the electrical wizard, called attention to the need for this change of direction when he wrote:

Spiritual power is a force which history clearly teaches has been the greatest force in the development of men. Yet we have been merely playing with it and have never really studied it as we have the physical forces. Some day people will learn that material things do not bring happiness, and are of little use in making people creative and powerful. Then the scientists of the world will turn their laboratories over to the study of spiritual forces which have hardly been scratched.

Somewhere amidst the atom, electrons and protons which make up the creative energies in which "we live and move and have our being" will be discovered the secrets of prayer, character, growth, thought, spirit and immortality. With open minds and open hearts we must put the spirit of man under the microscope.

—*Wilfred A. Peterson*

The One cannot be enumerated along with anything, nor even with uniqueness nor with ought else. The One cannot be enumerated in any way because *It is measure without itself being measured.*

—*Plotinus*

One who beholds My presence everywhere,
And all things dwelling equally in Me,
He never loses loving sight of Me,
Nor I of him, through all eternity.

That yogi finds security in Me,
Who, though his days be rushed and action-filled,
Is anchored inwardly, at rest in Me,
And worships Me in every living form.

That one, Arjuna, is the best of men,
And truest he, of yogis, whose heart feels
The joys of all, their pains, their searing griefs,
With equal care as though they were his own.

—*Bhagavad Gita*

He who knows the first vital thread binding all the things
formed in shape, colour and words, knows only the physical
form of the universe, and knows very little.

But he who goes deeper and perceives the string inside
the string, the thin web binding separate life forces with
cords of unity, knows the real entity.

Only he knows truly the mighty ommipotent and
omnipresent God, Who is within and beyond all formulated
entities of the vast universe. Penetrate deeper to know the
ultimate truth.

—*Atharva Veda*

Were one to live for four ages, nay, ten times more;
Were he to be known on the nine continents, and everyone
show him respect;
If he does not earn God's grace, he would not be noticed by
Him.
He would be a worm among worms and punished for his
sins (of not meditating on Him).

—*Japji*

79

A man whose mind is satiated in God acquires wisdom, consciousness and understanding;
He acquires the inner knowledge of all spheres of the universe;
He does not suffer the punishment of transmigration, and does not fear death, and achieves salvation.
Such is the result of meditation on immaculate God, if one worships Him with full concentration of mind.

A man whose mind is satiated with God is not obstructed in his path; and departs with honour and distinction.
He moves on the highway, and not the byways (which lead astray), and achieves intrinsic kinship with virtue.
Such is the result of meditation on immaculate God, if one worships him with full concentration of mind.

A man whose mind is satiated in God reaches (while alive) the gates of salvation; and saves his kith and kin;
He achieves communion with God, and saves his disciples (by showing them the true way), and does not wander in transmigration.
Such is the result of meditation on immaculate God, if one worships Him with full concentration of mind.

—*Japji*

Sequestered should he sit,
Steadfastly meditating, solitary,
His thoughts controlled, his passions laid away,
From every craving of possessions freed.

—*Bhagavad Gita*

Reason is not an end in itself but a tool for the individual to use in adjusting himself to the values and purposes of living which are beyond reason. Just as the teeth are intended to chew with, not to chew themselves, so the mind is intended to think with, not to worry about. The mind is an instrument to live with, not to live for.

—*Henry, C. Link*

Entering into the *samadhi* of purity, one obtains all-penetrating insight that enables one to become conscious of the absolute oneness of the universe.

—*Aushvaghosha*

Within the heart lies supreme affection, boundless enthusiasm, lasting peace, compassion like nectar. Muktananda, go there.

—*Swami Muktananda*

Meditation depends on the inclination to meditate, and on nothing else.

—*Swami Muktananda*

Seated amidst all is the most glorious, all-wise and vigilant Lord, breathing like a swan.
His mouth is immersed under the veil of cosmic vapours.
Bearing in His hand all might,
He abides and delegates His strength to the true seekers.
The sages realise Him through deep meditation and sincere devotion.

—*Rig Veda*

Taking as a bow the great weapon of the *Upanishad*,
One should put upon it an arrow sharpened by meditation.
Stretching it with a thought directed to the essence of that,
Penetrate that imperishable as the mark, my friend.

—*Mundaka Upanishad*

If we speak of the space-experience in meditation, we are dealing with an entirely different dimension.
.....In this space-experience the temporal sequence is converted into a simultaneous coexistence, the side-by-side existence of things....and this again does not remain static but becomes a living continuum in which time and space are integrated.

—*Lama Anagarika Govinda*

It is believed by most that time passes; in actual fact, it stays where it is. This idea of passing may be called time, but it is an incorrect idea, for since one sees it only as passing, one cannot understand that it stays just where it is.

—*J.Kennett*

Time, space, and causation are like the glass through which the Absolute is seen....In the Absolute there is neither time, nor space, nor causation.

—*S.Vivekananda, Jnana Yoga*

The stillness in stillness is not the real stillness. Only when there is stillness in movement can the spiritual rhythm appear which pervades heaven and earth.

—*Ts'ai-kent'an*

Meditation is the means of unification of the subject and object. It means that the mind is turned back upon itself.

—*Swami Vivekananda*

Matter and mind should be properly understood by those who meditate. For most people, matter is inert; and mind is active; but matter is a state of mind, and mind is a state of matter. You must clearly understand that matter and mind are two different states of one reality. The central core of the mind and the central core of matter in each case is energy, or *Shakti*.

—*Swami Satyanandaji*

Let us be silent, that we may hear the whispers of God.

—*Ralph Waldo Emerson*

Meditation is explosion and discovery. It is something that comes naturally when all positive and negative assertions and accomplishments have been understood and stopped away easily. It is total emptiness of the brain. It is emptiness that is essential: there is seeing only from emptiness; all virtues, not only social morality and respectability, spring from it.

—*J. Krishnamurti*

Wisdom comes to a man who meditates, acts and lives according to the true eternal laws of Nature.

—*Rig Veda*

Great are the rewards of contemplation. One who trains himself in the art of meditation will penetrate the heart of truth and discover great spiritual riches.

—*Buddhism*

Thinking of the great things of life results in greatness. If one would be good, he must contemplate the good. All virtues will be strengthened by meditating upon them. This, too, is the way to clearer understanding.

—*Christianity*

One should avoid bad, evil thoughts. He should at all times think that which is good. Careful consideration of the end as well as the beginning and middle will save one much trouble.

—*Confucianism*

One who does not meditate can have no steadiness nor peace. The great and the wise meditate constantly on the divine. This is the source of strength and the way to knowledge of the Supreme One.

—*Hinduism*

Contemplation is the means of obtaining stability of mind. Even though one is severely persecuted, he must obey the law of silent meditation.

—Jainism

Meditation brings understanding. One should contemplate God in all His greatness at all times. This is enjoyable and brings the greatest of peace and happiness. To meditate upon the Law of the Lord is the duty of all believers.

—Judaism

Meditate upon God and you will find peace. Meditation must be in humility and constant if one would reap its true rewards.

—Mohammedanism

Keep the plan and purposes of the Lord always in mind. Meditate upon them day and night. Then you will come to clear understanding.

—Zoroastrianism

The world's salvation commenced in God's heart, and is contained in the throb of every human heart that carries in it the beat of the heavenly pulse. And when our work is finished, the value that we have been to the world will have to be estimated by the amount of love-deposit we have been able to leave in the treasury of the world's life.

—Charles H. Parkhurst

Salvation is no bargain-counter product. We have to pay for it in full. Though God pays for the guilt of personal relations and freely offers to us full restoration to fellowship, we still have to pay for the consequences of our deeds in works of faith and love within the grace of God.

—Nels F.S. Ferre

84

The Practical Value of Meditation

A profitable pastime is to select a significant saying, ar meditate upon it for a few minutes until you have mad your own. By this simple means you can furnish your r with many beautiful and inspiring thoughts, which will be ready to serve you at times of need. The following thoughts will be of suggestive value in this respect: God is love. True knowledge is based on truth. Divine Mind is eternal. Right thinking is prayer. Truth, good, and beauty should each be sought for its own sake. Faith is always creative. Thrift of time brings ripeness of mind. Opinion of good men is but knowledge in the making. Books are a bloodless substitute for life. We live in an ascending scale when we live happily. An inspiration is a joy forever.

—*Unknown*

In the matter of man's salvation God is first. He comes to us self-invited—he names us by name—he isolates us from the crowd, and sheds upon us the sense of personal recognition—he pronounces the benediction, till we feel that there is a mysterious blessing on our house, and on our meal, and on our heart.

—*Frederick William Robertson*

Earth, with her thousand voices, praises God.
—*Samuel Taylor Coleridge*

Of all the ways of awakening inner reverence in man, the best is the contemplation of the works of God. Their transcendent greatness must inspire awe.

—*Elijah De Vidas*

We look at it and do not see it;
Its name is *The Invisible*.
We listen to it and do not hear it;
Its name is *The Inaudible*.
We touch it and do not find it;
Its name is *The Subtle*.
These three cannot be further inquired into,
And hence merge into one.
Going up high it is not bright, and coming down low, it is not dark,
Infinite and boundless, it cannot be given any name;
It reverts to nothingness.

—*Tao Te Ching*

That which cannot be expressed by speech but that by which speech is expressed: know that this indeed, not what is adored here, is the true *Brahman*.

—*The Upanishads*

When the soul that loves God searches into the nature of the Existent, it enters into an *invisible search*, from which the *chief benefit* which accrues to it is to comprehend that *God is incomprehensible and to know that he is invisible*.

—*Philo Judaeus*

RENUNCIATION

*The only thing you will take through
those pearly gates is what you've given
away.*

　　　　　　　　　　　—Marie Moore

That man alone is wise, of understanding steadfast and unwavering, whose senses are obedient to his discrimination. If one ponders on sense objects, there springs up attraction to them. From attraction grows desire. Desire, impatient for fulfilment, flames to anger. From anger there arises infatuation (the delusion that one object alone is worth clinging to, to the exclusion of all others). From infatuation ensues forgetfulness of the higher Self. From forgetfulness of the Self follows degeneration of the discriminative faculty. And when discrimination is lost, there follows the annihilation of one's spiritual life.

—Bhagavad Gita

Desire obscures even the wisdom of the wise. Their relentless foe it is, a flame never quenched.
Intellect, mind, and senses: These combined are referred to as the seat of desire. Desire, through them, deludes and eclipses the discrimination of the embodied soul.
O Arjuna, discipline your senses ! And having done so, work to destroy desire, annihilator of wisdom and of Self-realisation."

—Bhagavad Gita

If we would understand God, we must renounce our egoistic and ignorant human standards; or else ennoble and universalise them.

—Sri Aurobindo

And a man's foes shall be they of his own household.
He that loveth father or mother more than me is not worthy of me: and he that loveth son or daughter more than me is not worthy of me.
    And he that taketh not his cross, and followeth after me, is not worthy of me.
    He that findeth his life shall lose it: and he that loseth his life for my sake shall find it.

—Gospel of St. Mathew

We must learn to act without attachment. But it is rare for anyone untrained to reach the stage at which he is proof against disturbance by any act or anybody. This needs prodigiously hard work: and for God to be as present and to show as plainly to him at all times and in all company, that is for the expert and demands especially two things. One is that the man be closeted within himself where his mind is safe from images of outside things which remain external to him and alien as they are, cannot traffic or forgather with him or find any room in him at all. Secondly invention of the mind itself, ideas, spontaneous notions or images of things outside or whatever comes into his head, he must give no quarter to, on pain of scattering himself and being sold into multiplicity. His powers must all be trained to turn and face his inner self.

Thou dost object. "But one must turn outwards to do outward works: no work is wrought except in its own mode—True. But to the expert soul outward modes are not merely outward things: to the interior soul all things are modes of the Deity within.

—*Eckhart*

The foremost of your armies is that of Desire, the second is called Dislike.
The third is Hunger-thirst and the fourth is Craving.
The fifth is the army of Lethargy-laziness and the sixth is Fear.
The seventh is Doubt and the eight is Obstinacy-restlessness.
Then there are Material Gain, Praise. Honor, and Fame...
These, O Mara, are your forces, the attackers of the Evil One.
One less than a hero will not be victorious over them and attain happiness.

—*Sutta Nipata*

Blessed are they that mourn: for they shall be comforted.

Blessed are the meek: for they shall inherit the earth

Blessed are they which do hunger and thirst after righteousness: for they shall be filled.

Blessed are the merciful: for they shall obtain mercy

Blessed are the pure in heart: for they shall see God

Blessed are the peacemakers: for they shall be called the children of God.

Blessed are they which are persecuted for righteousness' sake: for their is the kingdom of heaven.

Blessed are ye, when men shall revile you, and persecute you, and shall say all manner of evil against you falsely, for my sake.

Rejoice, and be exceedingly glad: for great is your reward is heaven: for so persecuted they the prophets which were before you."

—*Gospel of St. Mathew*

At birth each of us has been given, by a wise Creator, the right of choice—the freedom to become what we want to become. This gift sets us high above the animal kingdom with their gift of instinct. In a true sense, we have been commissioned at birth as the captains of our own ship and the masters of our own soul. Most people forfeit their commissions—their priceless birthright. The vast majority of people remain ignorant of their powers because nowhere are they taught how to use them.

Instead of being the driver of our lives, we hand the reins or steering wheel over to our impulses, passions and moods. From that moment on we surrender this high prerogative that has been ours since birth.

To be morally free—to be more than an animal—man must be able to resist instinctive impulses. This can only be done by the exercise of self-control. Thus it is this power that constitutes the real distinction between a physical and a moral life, and that forms the primary basis of individual character.

Nine-tenths of the vicious desires that degrade society, and the crimes that disgrace it, would shrink into insignificance before the advance of valiant self-discipline and self-respect.

Moderation in all things, and regulating the actions only by the judgement, are the most eminent parts of wisdom. "He that ruleth his own spirit is greater than he that taketh a city."

To be free one must have command over himself.

Trust thyself; every breast vibrates to that iron string.

—_Ralph Waldo Emerson_

It is well to fix the thought in concerned effort: the man of wandering mind lies between the fangs of the Passions. It cannot wander if body and thought be in solitude: so it is well to forsake the world and put away vain imaginations.

—_Santi-deva_

Talk not of strength, till your heart has known
And fought with weakness through long hours alone.

Talk not of virtue, till your conquering soul
Has met temptation and gained full control

Boast not of garments, all unscorched by sin,
Till you have passed unscathed through fires within !

—_Unknown_

Grant us, O Master, Thy grace
To follow the good and the pure,
To rejoice in simple things,
To serve the poor in thought, word and deed,
To whisper not a word of hate or shame
To cast away the carnal self,
To speak no ill of others,
To have a mind at peace with all:

—_Unknown_

They who give away their substance in alms, by night and day, in private and in public, shall have their reward with their Lord: no fear shall come to them, neither shall they be put to grief.

—*Qur'an*

Ye men of mine, shun desire. If you shun desire, you will ascend to a level with the Gods. Every little yielding to anxiety is a step away from the natural heart of man. If one leaves the natural heart of man, he becomes a beast. That man should be made so is, to me, intolerable pain and unending sorrow.

—*Shintoism*

Leave the things of this world and come to Me daily and monthly with pure bodies and pure hearts. You will them enjoy paradise in this world and have all your desires accomplished.

—*Shintoism*

The depth of darkness to which you can descend and still live is an exact measure of the height to which you can aspire to reach.

—*Laurens Van der Post*

The blossom vanishes of itself as the fruit grows. So will your lower self vanish as the Divine grows in you.

—*Swami Vivekananda*

He cannot be comprehended by thoughts, even if one thinks of Him a hundred thousand times.
The quietitude of mind cannot be achieved by vow of silence, even if one goes in deep trance.
The fasting does not satiate the hunger for worldly goods, even if one has all the riches of the world.

Not one out of a hundred thousand devices and contrivances
works to achieve unity with Him.

How is the Truth, unity with God, to be attained ?
How is the veil of falsehood to be torn aside ?
This is to be done by submission to His *Hukum,*
Divine Order, which is ingrained in oneself.

—Japji

The five colours make man's eyes blind;
The five notes make his ears deaf;
The five flavours injure his palate;
Riding and hunting make his mind go mad.
Goods hard to come by serve to hinder his progress.
Hence the sage is for the belly and not the eye.
Therefore he discards the one and takes the other.

—Tao Te Ching 12

Yoga consist not in frequenting wild places, tombs and
cremation grounds.
Nor in falling into trances;
Nor lies it in wandering about to the world.
Nor in ritual bathing.
To live immaculate admidst the impurities of the world.
This is true *yoga* practice.

—Adi Granth

I renounce the honours to which the world aspires and
desires only to know the Truth.

—Socrates

PRAYER

If you pray, you will believe; if you believe, you will love; and if you love, you will serve.

—Mother Teresa

God Answers Prayer

I know not by what methods rare,
But this I know, God answers prayer,
I know that He has given His Word
Which tells me prayer is always heard.
And will be answered, soon or late.
And so I pray and calmly wait.

I know not if the blessing sought,
Will come in just the way I thought;
I leave my prayers with Him alone,
Whose will is wiser than my own,
Assured that He will grant my quest,
Or send an answer far more blest.

—*Eliza Hickok*

To those who meditate on Me as their Very Own, ever united
to Me by incessant worship, I make good their deficiencies
and render permanent their gains.

—*Bhagavad Gita*

Prayer is the heart of Religion and Faith
But how shall we pray ? What words shall convey
The yearnings of our miserable ignorant hearts
To the Knower of all ? Is it worthy of Him
Or of our spiritual nature to ask
For vanities, or even for such physical needs
As our daily bread ? The Inspired One
Taught us a Prayer that sums up our faith,
Our hope, and our aspiration in things that matter.
We think in devotion of God's name and His Nature;
We praise Him for His creation and His Cherishing care;
We call to mind the Realities, seen and unseen;
We offer Him worship and ask for His guidance;

95

And we know the straight from the crooked path
By the light of His grace that illumines the righteous.

—*Qur'an*

But when ye pray, use not vain repetitions, as the heathen do: for they think that they shall be heard for thier much speaking.

Be not ye therefore like unto them: for your Father knoweth what things ye have need of before ye ask him.

After this manner therefore pray ye: Our Father which art in heaven, Hallowed by Thy name.

Thy kingdom come. Thy will be done in earth, as it is in heaven.

Give us this day our daily bread.

And forgive us our debts, as we forgive our debtors.

And lead us not into temptation, but deliver us from evil: For Thine is the kingdom, and the power, and the glory, for ever. Amen.

For if ye forgive men their trespasses, your heavenly Father will also forgive you:

But if ye forgive not men thier trespasses, neither will your Father forgive your trespasses."

—*Gospel of St. Mathew*

Prayer is communion with God. Just as food is necessary for the nourishment of the physical body, prayer is equally necessary for the nourishment of the mind and the soul. Even for physical well being and sound health, prayer is very necessary. Whatever acts are done with an offering of prayer get submitted and transmitted in acts of worship.

Prayer elevates the mind, illumines the intellect, sublimates the senses, purifies the heart, awakens the soul-consciousness and helps to establish rapport with God.

—*Sathya Sai Baba*

The Kneeling Camel

The camel at the close of day
Kneels down, upon the sandy plain
To have his burden lifted off,
And rest again
My soul, thou too shouldst to thy knees
When daylight draweth to a close
And let thy Master lift thy load,
And grant repose

Else how canst thou tomorrow meet,
With all tomorrow's work to do,
If thou thy burden all the night
Dost carry through ?

The camel kneels at break of day
To have his guide replace his load,
Then rises up anew to take
The desert road.

So thou shouldst kneel at morning dawn
That God may give thy daily care,
Assured that He no load too great
Will make thee bear.

—*Anna Temple Whritney*

And when thou prayest, thou shall not be as the hypocrites
are: for they love to pray standing in the synagogues and in
the corners of the streets, that they may be seen of men. Verily
I say unto you, They have their reward.

But thou, when thou prayest, enter into thy closet, and
when thou hast shut thy door, pray to the Father which is in
secret; and thy Father which seeth in secret shall reward thee
openly.

—*Gospel of St. Mathew*

My debts are large, my failures great , my shame secret and heavy; yet when I come to ask for my good I quake in fear lest my prayer be granted.

—*Rabindranath Tagore*

The Power of Prayer

Lord, what a change within us one short hour
   Spent in Thy presence will avail to make !
   What heavy burdens from our bosoms take;
   What parched grounds refresh, as with a shower !

We kneel, and all around us seems to lower;
   We rise, and all, the distant and the near,
   Stands forth in sunny outline, brave and dear !
   We kneel, how weak ! We rise, how full of power !

Why, therefore, should we do ourselves this wrong
   Or others, that we are not always song;
   That we are ever overborne with care;
   That we should ever weak or heartless be,
   Anxious and troubled, when with us in prayer,
   And joy and strength and courage are with Thee ?

—*Richard Trench*

There are five prayers, five times for prayers and five names of them.

   The first should be truth, the second what is right, the third charity in God's name, the fourth good intentions, the fifth the praise and glory of God.
Give me the mind, O dear, that forgets Thee not
Give me the wisdom that I meditate on no one but Thee
And I praise Thee with every breath
And seek no other but the Guru's refuge, O dear!

—*Guru Nanak*

Prayer is the application of want to Him who alone can relieve it; the voice of sin to Him who alone can pardon it. It is the urgency of poverty, the prostration of humility, the fervency of penitence, the confidence of Trust. It is not eloquence, but earnestness; not figure of speech, but compunction of soul. It is the "Lord, save, I perish" of drowning Peter... It is not a mere conception of the mind, nor an effort of the intellect, nor an act of the memory, but an elevation of the soul towards its Maker. It is the devout breathing of a creature struck with a sense of its own misery and of the infinite holiness of Him whom it is addressing, experimentally convinced of its own emptiness and of the abundant fullness of God, of His readiness to hear, of His power to help, of His willingness to save... Prayer is might in itself as the most powerful means of resisting sin and advancing in holiness. It is above all might, as everything is which has the authority of scripture, the command of God, and the example of Christ.

—*Hannah More*

The average man prays to God with his mind only, not with all the fervour of his heart. Such prayers are too weak to bring any response. We should speak to the Divine Spirit with confidence and with a feeling of closeness, as to a father or a mother. Our relationship with God should be one of unconditional love. More than in any other relationship, we may rightfully and naturally demand a reply from Spirit in Its aspect as the Divine Mother. God is constrained to answer such an appeal; for the essence of a mother is love and forgiveness of her child, no matter how great sinner he may he.

—*Sri Sri Paramahansa Yogananda*

At the muezzin's call for prayer,
　The kneeling Faithful thronged the square,
And on *Pushkara's* lofty height
　The dark priest chanted *Brahma's* might.
Amid a monastery's weeds
　An old *Franciscan* told his beads,
While to the synagogue there come
　A jew, to praise *Jehovah's* name.

The one great God looked down and smiled
　And counted each his loving child;
For Turk and Brahmin, Monk and Jew
　Had reached Him through the Gods they knew.
　　　　　　　　　　—*Harry Romaine*

Leave this chanting and singing and telling of beads! Whom dost thou worship in this lonely dark corner of a temple with doors all shut? Open thine eyes and see thy God is not before thee!

He is where the tiller is tilling the hard ground and where the pathmaker is breaking stones. He is with them in the sun and in shower, and His garment is covered with dust. Put off thy holy mantle and even like Him come down on the dusty soil.

Deliverance? Where is this deliverance to be found? Our Master Himself has joyfuly taken upon Him the bonds of creation; He is bound with us all for ever.

Come out of thy meditations and leave aside thy flowers and incense. What harm is there if thy clothes become tattered and stained? Meet Him and stand by Him in toil and in sweat of thy brow.

　　　　　　　　　　—*Rabindranath Tagore*

No Prayer is Unanswered

Unanswered yet the prayer your lips have pleaded
   In agony of heart these many years?
Does faith begin to fail, is hope declining?
   And think you all in vain those falling tears?
Say not the Father has not heard your prayer;
   You shall have your desire, sometime, somewhere

Unanswered yet? tho' when you first presented
   This one petition at the Father's throne,
It seemed you could not wait the time of asking,
So anxious was your heart to have it done;
   If years have passed since then, do not despair,
For God will answer you sometime, somewhere.

Unanswered yet? but you are not unheeded;
   The promises of God forever stand;
To Him our days and years alike are equal;
   Have faith in God. It is your Lord's command.
Hold on to Jacob's angel, and your prayer
   Shall bring a blessing down sometime, somewhere,

Unanswered yet? Nay, do not say unanswered,
   Perhaps your part is not yet wholly done,
The work began when first your prayer was uttered,
   And God will finish what he has begun,
Keep incense burning at the shrine of prayer,
   And glory shall descend sometime, somewhere.

Unanswered yet? Faith cannot be unanswered;
   Her feet are firmly planted on the Rock;
Amid the wildest storms she stands undaunted,
   Nor quails before the loudest thunder shock.
She knows Omnipotence has heard her prayer,
   And cries, "It shall be done sometime, somewhere".

           —*Ophelia Guyan Browning*

Your Church and Mine

You go to your church, and I'll go to mine,
But let's walk along together;
Our Father has built them said by side,
So let's walk along together.
The road is rough and the way is long,
But we'll help each other over;
You go to your church and I'll go to mine,
But let's walk along together.

You go to your church, and I'll go to mine,
But let's walk along together;
Our heavenly Father is the same,
So let's walk along together.
The chimes of your church ring loud and clear,
They chime with the chimes of my church;
You go to your church and I'll go to mine,
But let's walk along together.

You go to your church, and I'll go to mine,
But let's walk along together;
Our heavenly Father loves us all,
So let's walk along together.
The Lord will be at my church today,
And He'll be at your church too;
You go to your church, and I'll go to mine,
But let's walk along together.

—*Phillips H. Lord*

We cannot speak of God, He is beyond compare,
And so we can adore Him best with silent prayer.

—*Angelus Silesius*

Two men knelt down to pray.

Said one: "Give what I want, O Lord. Prosper me in business. Listen to my pleadings, and make my way of life easy".

This man stood up unblessed, for God heard him not.

Said the other: "O Lord, Thou understandest my thought afar off, and art acquainted with all my ways. Search me, O God, and know my heart; try me and know my thoughts. See if there be any wickedness in me, and lead me in the way everlasting".

This man rose and went forth to bless others, and in that blessing found joy and peace.

—Unknown

My Church

My church has but on temple,
　Wide as the world is wide,
Set with a million stars,
　Where a million hearts abide,
My church has no creed to bar
　A single brother man
But says, "Come thou and worship"
　To every one who can.
My church has no roof nor walls
　Nor floors save the beautiful God –
For fear, I would seem to limit
　The love of illimitable God.

—Unknown

Prayer is the turning of the mind and heart to God. To pray is to stand in awareness before God, to see him constantly and to talk with him in hope and fear.

—Saint Demetrius of Rostov

Pray with a Sincere Heart

When the mind and speech unite in earnestly asking for a thing that prayer is answered. Of no avail are the prayers of that man who says with his mouth, "These are all Thine, O Lord !" and at the same time thinks in his heart that all of them are his. Be not a traitor in your thoughts. Be sincere; act according to your thoughts; and you shall surely succeed. Pray with a sincere and simple heart, and your prayers will be heard.

—*Sri Ramakrishna*

How often we look upon God as our last and feeblest resource ! We go to Him because we have nowhere else to go. And then we learn that the storms of life have driven us, not upon the rocks, but into the desired havens.

—*George MacDonald*

How to pray

In quiet and calm solitude
Talk to yourself, about you
Don't be shy, don't hold back anything
Your innermost secrets remain secret with you
Talk about your embarrassments and achievements
Your dreams and aspirations fulfilled or not yet fulfilled;
Talk about your weakneses and strengths
Yor failures and successes–your aims and ambitions;
Talk about your giving and getting love
Affections, hates and rebuffs–your dilemmas and delusions;
Talk about chances missed or cashed
Battles, wars and conflicts–within and without
Talk with your heart and soul
To your heart and soul;
Talk to yourself
You are praying.

—*S.N. Mehta*

Let me pray not to be sheltered from dangers
    but to be fearless in facing them
Let me not beg for the stilling of my pain,
    but for the heart to conquer it.
Let me not look for allies in life's battlefield,
    but to my own strength.
Let me crave not in anxious fear to be saved,
    but hope for the patience to win my freedom.
Grant me that I may not be a coward, feeling
    your mercy in my success alone; but let me
    find the grasp of your hand in failure.

                        —*Rabindranath Tagore*

This is the gist of all worship—to be pure and to do good to others. He who sees Siva in the poor, in the weak, and in the diseased, really worships Siva, and if he sees Siva only in the image, his worship is but preliminary. He who has served and helped one poor man seeing Siva in him—without thinking of his caste, creed or race, or anything—with him Siva is more pleased than with the man who sees Him only in temples.

                        —*Swami Vivekananda*

This Prayer I Make

This prayer I make,
Knowing that Nature never did betray
The heart that loved her;' tis her privilege,
Through all the years of this our life, to lead
From joy to joy: for she can so inform
The mind that is within us, so impress
With quietness and beauty, and so feed
With lofty thoughts, that neither evil tongues,
Rash judgments, nor the sneers of selfish men,

Nor greetings where no kindness is, nor all
The dreary intercourse of daily life,
Shall e'er prevail against us, or disturb
Our cheerful faith, that all which we behold
Is full of blessings.

—*William Wordsworth*

The World is Better That I Lived Today

Let me today do something that will take
   A little sadness from the world's vast store,
And may I be so favored as to make
   Of joy's too scanty sum a little more.

Let me not hurt, by any selfish deed
   Or thoughtless word, the heart of foe or friend.
Nor would I pass unseeing worthy need,
   Or sin by silence when I should defend.

However meager by my worldly wealth,
   Let me give something that shall aid my kind—
A word of courage, or a thought of health
   Dropped as I pass for troubled hearts to find.

Let me tonight look back across the span
   Twixt dawn and dark, and to my conscience say—
Because of some good act to beast or man—
   "The world is better that I lived today."

—*Ella Wheeler Wilcox*

When thou prayest, rather let thy heart be without words,
than thy words without heart.

—*John Bunyan*

Prayer for the New Year

I ask not now for wisdom, for I find
  I do not use the little that I have;
Nor do I ask for power, for I fear
  The brute in me, that uses power as a club;
Nor riches, for I know full well that I
  Receive all that I earn, and maybe more.
I asked for these things once, in years gone by,
  And, in a measure, they have all been mine;
Each gift I craved was granted unto me
  As all things that we crave are granted from
  your store—
But if you have a face, Great Power, I know you smiled
  As from that store you gave the thing I craved,
For well you knew it would not fill my heart
  Nor make for beauty in my stupid hands.
So now, with clearer vision and a humbler heart
  I come to beg for that one precious boon—
Which is, I think the greatest gift of all—
  Help me to be kind!
Help me to be kind in motive and in deed,
  Help me be kind in my most secret thought,
In every touch I make on other lives,
  In every contact which they press on me.
Cleanse all the stinging rancor from my wit,
  Purge me of envy, greed and smug self-righteousness.
Make me remember only my own weakness, my own
  sin,
  When fools and sinners ask some boon of me.

Help me be kind!
  Not with the patronizing pity that's a lash
At self-respect, nor with a pride

That crushes those who show their need to me,
But with the constant knowledge that whate'er I have
    Of strength or money, wit or cleverness,
Belongs to them as much as it belongs to me.
    For all of it has come from out your store,
And those who give or take are brothers in your sight.
    And when I meet with scorn and ridicule,
When I am tricked by my own malice or stupidity
    And stand ashamed, besmirched before the sneering
    eyes of man,
Help me to keep my spirit sweet in that dark hour,
    Hold back my temper, make me tolerant and sane
To those that hurt me, as to those that I might hurt
    Help me be kind!
Great Power, who made me from the common clay,
    Yet breathed into that clay a flash of godlike fire,
Breathe now again, to light me through the year, and
warm
    My cold, hard spirit with that pure white ray of your
    own kindness.

—*Elsie Robinson*

Let me be a Giver

God, let me be a giver, and not one
    Who only takes and takes unceasingly;
God, let me give, so that not just my own,
    But others' lives as well, may richer be.

Let me give out whatever I may hold
    Of what material things life may be heaping,
Let me give raiment, shelter, food, or gold
    If these are, through Thy bounty, in my keeping.

But greater than such fleeting treasures, may
  I give my faith and hope and cheerfulness,
Belief and dreams and joy and laughter gay
  Some lonely soul to bless.
—Mary Carolyn Davies

Beware of the plea of the oppressed, for he asks God Most High only for his due, and God does not keep one who has a right from receiving what is his due.
—Hadith of Baihaqui

You are fortunate as you have got this human body. Pray to the Lord as much as you can. You must labour hard. It is difficult to attain anything without labour. Some time must be daily set apart for prayer and spiritual practices even though one is in the midst of worldly activities.

To pray to God and meditate on Him for even two minutes with full concentration is better than doing so for long hours without that.
—Sri Saradamani Devi

Keep me from bitterness. It is so easy
To nurse sharp bitter thoughts each dull dark hour !
Against self-pity, Man of sorrow, defend me,
With Thy deep sweetness and Thy gentle power.
And out of all this hurt of pain and heartbreak
Help me to harvest a new sympathy
For suffering human kind, a wiser pity
For those who lift a heavier cross with Thee.
—Unknown

A child is born through the rending of the womb;
A man is born through the rending of the world.
The call to prayer signalizes both kinds of birth,
The first is uttered by the lips, the second of the very soul.
—Mahomed Iqbal

O God of love, we yield Thee thanks for whatsoever Thou hast given us richly to enjoy: for health and vigour, for the love and care of home, for joys of friendship, and for every good gift to happiness and strength. We praise thee for all Thy servants who by their example for encouragement have helped us on our way, and for every vision of Thyself which Thou hast ever given us in sacrament or prayer; and we humbly beseech Thee that all these Thy benefits we may use to Thy service and to the glory of Thy holy Name; through Jesus Christ, Thy Son, our Lord. AMEN.

—*Prayers Old and New*

This is my prayer to Thee, my Lord, strike, strike at the root of penury in my heart.

Give me the strength lightly to bear my joys and sorrows.

Give me the strength to make my love fruitful in service.

Give me the strength never to disown the poor or bend my knees before insolent might.

Give me the strength to raise my mind high above daily trifles.

And give me the strength to surrender my strength to Thy will with love.

—*Rabindranath Tagore*

The only way truly to pray is to approach alone the One who is Alone. To contemplate that One, we must withdraw into the inner soul, as into a temple, and be still.

—*Plotinus*

He who rises from prayer a better man, his prayer is answered.

—*The Talmud*

He prayeth best who loveth best
All things both great and small;
For the dear God who loveth us,
He made and loveth all.

—*Samuel Taylor Coleridge*

The heavens are wide, exceedingly wide.
The earth is wide, very, very wide.
From time immemorial the God of old bids us all
Abide by his injunctions.
Then shall we get whatever we want, be it white or red.
It is God, the Creator, the Gracious One.
Good morning to you, God, good morning.
I am learning; let me succeed.

—*Akan of Ghana*

Father of Light! great God of Heaven!
    Hear'st thou the accents of despair?
Can guilt like man's be e'er forgiven?
    Can vice atone for crimes by prayer?

—*George Gordon, Lord Byron*

REALISATION

> — *Man becomes God, and all human activity reaches highest and noblest when it succeeds in bringing body, heart and mind into touch with the spirit.*
>
> —Sri Aurobindo

A Bag of Tools

Isn't it strange that princes and kings,
  And clowns that caper in sawdust rings,
And common folks, like you and me
  Are builders for Eternity.

To each is given a bag of tools,
  A shapeless mass and a book of rules,
And each must make ere life has flown
  A stumbling block or a stepping stone.
                              —*R.L. Sharpe*

Let chastity be the Smithy, patience the Smith,
Understanding the Anvil, knowledge the Tool,
Discipline the Bellows, austerity the Fire,
Devotion the Pot, immortality the Mould;
Thus in the mint of Truth, His Name is coined.
Those who catch His sight, and find acceptance,
  succeed in their toil.
They, by His grace, achieve salvation.
                              —*Adi Granth Japji*

Thou canst not see Me with mortal eyes.
Therefore I now give thee the sight divine.
Behold, My Supreme Power of *Yoga*! With these words, the
exalted Lord of *Yoga* revealed Himself to Arjuna in His
infinite Form.
                              —*Bhagavad Gita*

No man hath seen God at any time;
The only begotten son, which is in the bosom
Of the Father, he hath declared Him.
                              —*Gospel of St. John*

Humbleness, truthfulness, and harmlessness,
Patience and honor, reverence for the wise.
Purity, constancy, control of self,
Contempt for sense-delights, self-sacrifice,
Perception of the certainty of ill
In birth, old age, and frail mortality,
Disease, the ego's suffering, and sin;
Detachment, lightly holding thoughts of home,
Children, and wife—those ties which bind
    most men;
An ever-tranquil heart, heedless of good
Or adverse fortune, with the will upraised
To worship Me alone, unceasingly;
Loving deep solitude, and shunning noise
Of foolish crowds; calm focus on the Self
Perceived within and in Infinity:
These qualities reveal true Wisdom, Prince.
All that is otherwise is ignorance!

—*Bhagavad Gita*

The master said, 'Everything that exists is God. The pupil understood it literally, but not in the right spirit. While he was passing through the street he met an elephant. The driver shouted aloud from his high place. 'Move away ! Move away!' The pupil argued in his mind 'Why should I move away? I am God, so is the elephant God; what fear has God of himself? Thinking thus, he did not move. At last the elephant took him up in his trunk and dashed him aside. He was hurt severely, and going back to his master, he related the whole adventure. The master said: 'All right. You are God, the elephant is God also, but God in the shape of the elephant-driver was warning you from above. Why did you not pay heed to his warnings?'

—*Sri Ramakrishna*

How can the soul's self-conviction be fitly
Expressed, except by types of tremendous
Cataclysms in nature, and still more by tremendous
Searching in the heart of man ? These want
Deep pondering. When once the spiritual Dawn
Has "breathed away" the Darkness of the Night,
The Vision Glorious clears all doubts,
And brings us face to face with Truth.
The highest Archangel in heaven is sent
By God to bring these truths to men
Through their Apostle. God's Grace flows freely:
We have but to tune our Will to His,—
The ever-loving Righteous God.

—Qur'an

To acquire the power to attain the Infinite, one must first
know the finite and let oneself be guided by it. As long as the
soul is identified with the body it is indispensable to let
oneself be guided by what the rules enjoin or proscribe.

—Ananda Moyi

To know the real Self to be one's own is the greatest attainment
according to the Scriptures and reasoning. To know wrongly
the non-Self such as the ego, etc., to be the Self is no attainment
at all. One, therefore, should renounce this misconception of
taking the non-Self for the Self.

—Sri Sankaracharya

Every man whose heart is free from the perturbations of
doubt, knows with certitude that there is no being save One
alone. The word "I" belongs rightly to none but God.

—Gulschen-i-Raz

Arjuna said, 'Those who, ever steadfast, worship Thee as devotees, and those who contemplate Thee as the immortal, unmanifested Spirit—which group is the better versed in *yoga*?'

The blessed Lord replied: 'Those who, fixing their minds on Me, adore Me, ever united to Me through supreme devotion, are in My eyes the perfect knowers of *yoga*.

'Those whose strict aim is union with the Unmanifested choose a more difficult way; arduous for embodied being is the path of dedication to the Absolute.'

—*Bhagavad Gita*

The kingdom of God cometh not by observation, Neither shall they say, 'Look here!' or 'Look there!' For behold, the kingdom of God is within you.

—*Gospel of Luke*

The first step upwards is when we recognise ourselves as the children of God; the last step is when we realise ourselves as the One—the *Atman*.

—*Swami Vivekananda*

Forms vanish, rituals fly away, books are superceded; images, temples, churches, religions and sects, countries and nationalities—all these little limitations and bondages fall off by their own nature from him who knows his love of God.

—*Swami Vivekananda*

The greatest thing in th world is not so much where we are, but in what direction we are moving.

—*Oliver Wendell Holmes*

What lies behind us and what lies before us are small matters when compared to what lies within us.

—*Ralph Waldo Emerson*

In his higher nature, man is limitless. In the realm of mind, of character and of spirit there are no limitations save those which we impose upon ourselves; and no man reflects deeply without realising that the possibilities of growth in his true and higher being are practically infinite. This thought should arouse within one a profound sense of his instrinsic worth and greatness, as well as a deep reverence for himself because of his latent possibilities.

When one is thus awakened to a sense of his limitless possibilities the great need is the knowledge of the laws that make for growth and development.

Within each of us are hidden resources, which few have developed, capable of making us a power in the world. At birth we were equipped by an all-wise Creator with a mind of unlimited potential. If we are to derive strength and power out of the human mind, then, like the muscle, it must be put to use, it must be developed.

You must know yourself in order to know your powers, and not until you know them can you use them wisely and fully.

—*Anonymous*

Sometime

Sometime, when all life's lessons have been learned,
And sun and stars for ever more have set,
The things our weak judgment here have spurned,
The things o'er which we grieved with lashes wet,
Will flash before us out of life's dark night,
As stars shine most in deeper tints of blue;
And we shall see how all God's plans are right,
And how what seemed reproof was love most true.

And we shall see how, while we frown and sigh,
God's plans go on as best for you and me;

117

How, when we called, He heeded not our cry,
Because His wisdom, to the end could see.
And e'en as prudent parents disallow
Too much of sweet to craving babyhood,
So God, perhaps, is keeping from us now
Life's sweetest things, because it seemeth good.

And if, sometimes, commingled with life's wine,
We find the wormwood, and rebel and shrink,
Be sure a wiser hand than your or mine
Pours out the potion for our lips to drink;
And if some friend you love is lying low,
Where human kisses cannot reach his face,
Oh, do not blame the loving Father so,
But wear your sorrow with obedient grace.

And you shall shortly know that lengthened breath
Is not the sweetest gift God sends His friend,
And that, sometimes, the sable pall of death
Conceals the fairest boon His love can send;
If we could push ajar the gates of life,
And stand within, and all God's workings see,
We could interpret all this doubt and strife,
And for each mystery could find a key.

But not today. Then be content, poor heart;
God's plans, like lilies pure and white, unfold;
We must not tear the close-shut leaves apart,
Time will reveal the chalices of gold.
And if, through patient toil, we reach the land
Where tired feet, with sandals loosed, may rest,
When we shall clearly see and understand,
I think we will say, "God knew the best".

—*May Riley Smith*

The people that walked in darkness have seen a great light...
they that dwell in the land of the shadow of death, upon them
hath the light shined.

—The book of Prophet Isaih

For whom
That darkness of the soul is chased by light,
Splendid and clear shines manifest the Truth
As if a Sun of Wisdom sprang to shed
Its beams of light.

—Bhagavad Gita

Say not ye, There are yet four months, and then come the
harvest ?
Behold, I say unto you, Lift up your eyes, and look on the
field; for
They are white already to harvest.

—Gospel of St. John

Find the eternal object of your quest within your soul.
Enough have you wandered during the long period of your
quest !

Dark and weary must have been the ages of your
searching in ignorance and groping in helplessness.

At last when you turn your gaze inward, suddenly you
realise that the bright light of faith and lasting Truth was
shining around you.

With rapturous joy, you find the soul of the universe,
the eternal object of your quest.

Your searching mind at last finds the object of search
within your own heart.

Your inner vision is illuminated by this new realisation.

—Yajur Veda

I now realise the presence of the Almighty Lord, the universal entity, the one who is self-illuminated and radiant like the sun.

He is beyond all darkness; with this realisation, now I fear not even death.

I proclaim, this is the path, the only path to salvation, to the goal of life, the eternal bliss.

—*Yajur Veda*

When a lump of salt dissolves in the ocean it gives up its saltness and becomes the ocean. When identification with the body is dissolved, man becomes God.

—*Swami Muktananda*

Man is an unfinished creature towards his own caricature of man-to-be, and the whole purpose... is to accelerate the speed of evolution so that man can evolve faster and come to a stage of realisation of the ultimate reality when he will realise the basic lesson which every one of us has to learn, and it can never be learnt too soon — the basic lesson that we are all children of the same God; of ONE single creator.

—*Nani Palkhivala*

It is the 'same God, and the different realisations are only degrees and differences of vision.

—*Swami Vivekananda*

He that falls into sin is a man; that grieves at it is a saint; that boasts of it is a devil.

—*Thomas Fuller*

The One cannot be enumerated along with anything, nor even with uniqueness nor with ought else. The One cannot be enumerated in any way because *I is measure without itself being measured.*

—*Plotinus*

What is true of the relation between two men is not true of the relation of man to God: that the longer they live together and the better they get to know each other, the closer do they come to one another. *The very opposite is true in relation to God: the longer one lives with Him, the more infinite He becomes—and the smaller one becomes oneself.* Alas, as a child it seemed as though God and man could play together. Alas, in youth one dreamed that if one really tried with all the passion of a man in love the relationship might yet be brought into being. Alas, as a man one discovers how infinit God is, and the infinite distance.

—*Soren Kierkegaard*

Canst thou find the Almighty to perfection? No, not only because the power and wisdom He has manifested in the structure of the Creation that I behold is to me incomprehensible, but because even this manifestation, great as it is, is probably but a small display of the immensity of power and wisdom, by which millions of other worlds, to me invisible by their distance, were created and continue to exist.

—*Thomas Paine*

By continually seeking to know and being continually thrown back with a deepened conviction of the impossibility of knowing, we may keep alive the consciousness that is alike our highest wisdom and our highest duty to regard that through which all things exist as The Unknowable.

—*Herbert Spencer*

Compared to the vast oceanic volume of the unknown spiritual facts, what is all our own material knowledge before the immensity of that which is to come, the spiritual, the unknown, the immensity of being and facts around us of which we cannot possibly take any cognizance.

—*Walt Whitman*

God hath not made a Creature that can comprehend Him; 'tis a privilege of His own nature. *I AM THAT I AM*, was His own definition unto Moses; and 'twas a short one, to confound mortality, that darest question God, or ask Him what He was.

—*Sir Thomas Browne*

The "Name" which cannot be defined is turned into a definition. The meaning of the Sacred Name is precisely this: I am the Mysterious One, and I will remain so; I AM THAT I AM the Incomparable, therefore I cannot be defined nor named.

—*Emil Brunner*

God cannot be inferred in anything—in nature, say, as its author, or in history as its master, or in the subject as the self that is thought in it. Something else is not "given" and God then elicited from it; but God is the Being that is directly, most nearly, and lastingly, over against us, that may properly only be addressed, not expressed.

—*Martin Buber*

As no man knows the place of the soul, so no man knows the place of God. So let the soul, of which no man knows the place, praise God, who is exalted above His world, and whose "place" no man knows.

—*The Midrash*

What is the last end? It is the mystery of the darkness of the eternal Godhead which is unknown and never shall be known. Therein God abides to Himself unknown.

—*Meister Eckhart*

Our powers are so far from conceiving the divine height that, of the works of our creator, those best bear his stamp, and are most his, which we understand least.

—*Michel Eyquem De Montaigne*

He who is the self of all beings and the
   salvation of all beings,
About whose path even the heavenly powers
   are in confusion,
Seeking the track of the trackless,
As one cannot find the path of the birds in the air.

—The Upanishads

For what man knows the counsel of God?
Or who shall conceive what the Lord wills?
For the thoughts of mortals are timorous,
And our purposes are prone to fail.
And with difficulty do we divine the things of the earth
And the things close at hand do we discern with labor;
But the things in heaven who can trace out?

—The Old Testament Apocrypha

No organism corresponds completely to the Idea that lies at
its root; behind everyone the higher Idea is hidden. That is
my God, that is the God we all seek after and hope to find, but
we can only feel Him, we cannot see Him.

—Johann Wolfgang Von Goethe

Why should man go about seeking God? He is in thy heart-
beats and thou knowest it not; thou wert in error in seeking
Him outside thyself.

—Vivekananda

By the assemblage of all that is exalted and all that is base
man was always the most astonishing of mysteries.

—Farid-uddin Attar

There is only one temple in the universe and that is the body of man. Nothing is holier than this noble form. To bow down before man is a homage offered to this revelation in the flesh. We touch heaven when we lay our hand on a human body.

—Novalis

And yet, O the happiness of being man and of being able to recognise the way of the Truth and by following it to attain the goal.

—Gyokai

The sage's quest is for himself, the quest of the ignorant for the other than himself.

—Confucius

If anyone asks what is the shortest and surest way of disposing ourselves to advance continually in the spiritual life, I shall reply that it is to remain carefully self-gathered within, for it is there properly that one sees the gleam of the true light.

—Tauler

Our true glory and true riches are within.

—Seneca

It is when we seek for the things which are within us that quest leads to discovery.

—Meng Tse

The spirit constructs its own abode; directed falsely from the beginning it thinks in erroneous ways and engenders its own distress. Thought creates for itself its own suffering.

—Fa-ken-pi-u

Intelligence is worth more than all the possessions in the world.

—*Minokhired*

As the musician knows how to tune his lyre, so the wise man knows how to set his mind in tune with all minds.

—*Demophilus*

The mind is a clear and polished mirror and our continual duty is to keep it pure and never allow dust to accumulate upon it.

—*Hindu saying*

The Eternal is seen when the mind is at rest. When the sea of the mind is troubled by the winds of desire, it cannot reflect the Eternal and all divine vision is impossible.

—*Ramakrishna*

The power of the human intelligence is without bounds; it increases by concentration: that is the secret.

—*Vivekananda*

BEYOND DEATH

*Death is a change of address or P.O.
Box Number.*
                    —Unknown

*The human soul is eternal and
immortal, perfect and infinite, and death
means only a change of centre from one
body to another.*
                    —Swami Vivekananda